Ask the SCIENCE EXPERT

Written by
Pam Walker

Inside illustration by
Kathryn Marlin

Cover illustration by
Jeff Van Kanegan

Photo credits © Digital Stock Corporation and Corel Corporation

Publisher
Instructional Fair • TS Denison
Grand Rapids, MI 49544

ISBN: 0-7424-0138-3
Ask the Science Expert
Copyright © 2001 Instructional Fair • TS Denison
a Division of Instructional Fair Group, Inc.
3195 Wilson Dr. NW
Grand Rapids, Michigan 49544

To the Teacher

The format used in most science activities and experiments does not always fascinate middle school students. An interesting and unique approach to experimentation is sometimes all that is needed to capture the attention of the young learner.

Ask the Science Expert uses a unique approach to presenting the science problem of each experiment. The problem that students are asked to solve is presented in the form of an "Ask the Science Expert" advice column. This is followed by background information addressed to students about the topic being discussed. Following the background is a set of Prelab Research Questions in which students must rely on their powers of research to locate the answers. After completing the Prelab Research Questions, students engage in an experiment to help them determine the proper response to the problem stated in the beginning advice column.

Once the experiment is complete, students are armed with the information that will allow them to respond appropriately to the problem statement. The student now becomes the science expert and is ready to provide advice for the person who posed the original question. Students then write the conclusion statement in a format of one or two paragraphs in an advice column box addressing the original question.

This book includes both physical and life science activities. It allows students to use problem-solving and research skills to reach a conclusion. The advice-column format captures the attention of the student. The student's response makes use of good writing skills that reflect his or her conclusions to the experiment. An answer key at the back of the book provides information for the teacher, sample data tables and procedures, and probable conclusion statements.

Table of Contents

Teeth in Trouble

Dear Science Expert,

I go to the dentist's office every six months to get my teeth cleaned. I am 25 years old, but every time I go to the dental hygienist, she wants to treat my teeth with fluoride. I thought this was a children's treatment, but she said my mouth is very acidic and it is causing my teeth to develop cavities.

I have at least one cavity each time I get my teeth cleaned. She and my dentist think these fluoride treatments along with using a fluoride gel each day may eliminate my cavities. My insurance does not cover the cost of the fluoride treatments. Do you think it is worth the expense? Does fluoride really help prevent tooth decay?

Sincerely,
Cavity Prone

Procedure

1. Read the Background Information: Teeth in Trouble: Tooth Decay and the Environment.

2. Answer the Prelab Research Questions.

3. Follow the steps of the procedure to conduct the experiment following the Prelab Research Questions so that you become the science expert.

4. Acting as the science expert, write a response to Cavity Prone's letter.

Tooth Decay and the Environment

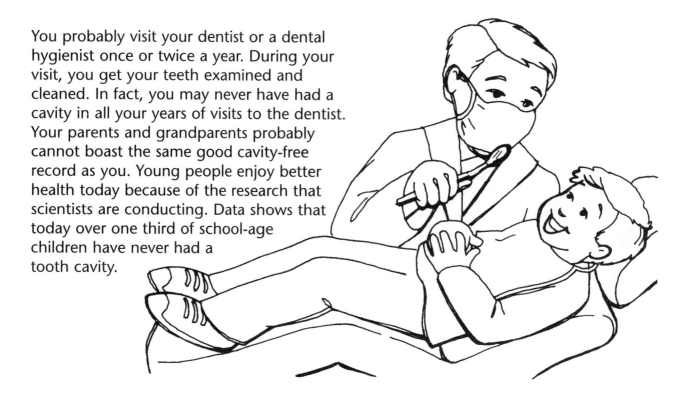

You probably visit your dentist or a dental hygienist once or twice a year. During your visit, you get your teeth examined and cleaned. In fact, you may never have had a cavity in all your years of visits to the dentist. Your parents and grandparents probably cannot boast the same good cavity-free record as you. Young people enjoy better health today because of the research that scientists are conducting. Data shows that today over one third of school-age children have never had a tooth cavity.

What is different today from when your parents were children? Your parents were told to brush their teeth after meals and eat a good diet just like you were. They may have even been told to floss their teeth daily. The difference between today and then is the presence of fluoride in our water supply.

Bacteria that gets into the mouth produce enzymes and acids. These acids have the ability to split proteins. This can destroy the protein matrix of the enamel, resulting in tooth decay. The presence of fluoride on tooth enamel can protect the tooth from decay, because fluoride on tooth enamel is not easily dissolved by the acids in your mouth. This results in more cavity-free checkups.

Name _____

Prelab Research Questions

Conduct library research to answer the following questions.

1. What is the difference between deciduous and permanent teeth? _____
   _____
   _____

2. What is the name of the part of the tooth that lies below the enamel?_____

3. When a person has a cavity that invades the pulp cavity, infection can eventually spread to bone and through the root canal. What material does the pulp cavity contain that allows this to happen? _____
   _____

4. The teeth, like the bones of the body, contain two vital substances or elements. Name these two elements that are essential to their structural strength. _____
   _____

5. How many permanent teeth do most adults have? _____

6. How many deciduous teeth do most people have? _____

7. What is malocclusion of the teeth? _____
   _____

Does Fluoride Protect From Acids?

Purpose: Determine whether fluoride protects the tooth from acids.

Materials Needed:
Two eggshells (simulate human teeth)
Vinegar (an acid)
Two beakers
Fluoride gel (Stannous fluoride toothpaste)
Graduated cylinder
Two cotton swabs
Two pieces of waxed paper
Masking tape

Procedure:

1. Use a cotton swab to completely cover one eggshell with a layer of fluoride gel. The eggshell is composed of the same material that composes your teeth.

2. Place the prepared eggshell on a piece of waxed paper labeled A. Place a second eggshell, which you do not cover with gel, on a piece of waxed paper labeled B.

3. Leave both eggshells undisturbed for 24 hours.

4. The next day, use masking tape to label one beaker A and another beaker B.

5. Place the eggshell covered with fluoride gel in the bottom of beaker A and the other eggshell in beaker B.

6. Use a graduated cylinder to add 100 mL of vinegar to both beakers (see Figure 1).

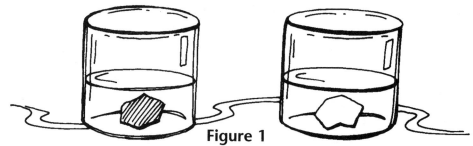

Figure 1

7. After 30 minutes in the vinegar, remove both eggshells from the beakers and observe the appearance of the shells. Note any changes that have occurred in the appearance of the shells.

Letter to **Cavity Prone** *from the Science Expert*

Use the information that you collected in the experiment that you just performed to write a response to Cavity Prone's questions. Your letter should use complete sentences, correct spelling, and contain conclusions drawn from your experiment. You are now the science expert. Your letter should be creative and at least one to two paragraphs long.

Dear Cavity Prone,

Sincerely,
Science Expert

Little Beings

Dear Science Expert,

I have been reading about decomposers in my science books recently. It is scary to think where we would be if there were no decomposers on earth. I can't imagine all the dead plants and animals just lying there in the forest and nothing to break them down into nutrients for the soil. I guess without decomposers the soil might become barren and plant growth would be reduced. I can see how that would affect animals and especially humans.

I was wondering if decomposers were affected by pollution. I know that pollution makes fish and birds sick and can even kill them. Salt runoff from roads in northern states and detergent runoff from homes and industry are two common types of pollutants. What effect do these pollutants have on decomposers, such as yeast? I think I read somewhere that yeast undergoes respiration like other living things. Can you do a little test and let me know how yeast responds to pollutants, such as salt and soap?

Sincerely,
Fan of Fungi

Procedure

1. Read the Background Information: Little Beings: Yeast and Pollution.

2. Answer the Prelab Research Questions.

3. Follow the steps of the procedure to conduct the experiment following the Prelab Research Questions so that you become the science expert.

4. Acting as the science expert, write a response to Fan of Fungi's letter.

Yeast and Pollution

Yeast is a one-celled organism that belongs to the classification kingdom called *fungi*. Yeasts are one of over 100,000 different kinds of fungi. All fungi lack chlorophyll, the pigment necessary for food-making. Therefore, fungi cannot make their own food. As yeasts feed, they break materials into smaller parts. If the material they are feeding on is dead, this process is called *decay*. All types of organisms that cause decay are given the name *decomposers*.

Decomposers are very important to life on earth. Since living things die constantly, decomposers help to break the dead organisms into smaller parts through decay. These smaller parts are reused by plants and animals. Without decomposers, dead materials would stack up forever on the earth and lock up important nutrients the soil needs for plant growth.

Under the right conditions, yeasts form living colonies. You may have noticed yeast in a package the last time you were in the grocery store. Once warm water is added to the contents of the package, the yeasts become a living colony. As the yeasts are activated by water, they begin to undergo respiration and release carbon dioxide gas. The addition of sugar to the yeasts gives them a food source on which to grow and flourish.

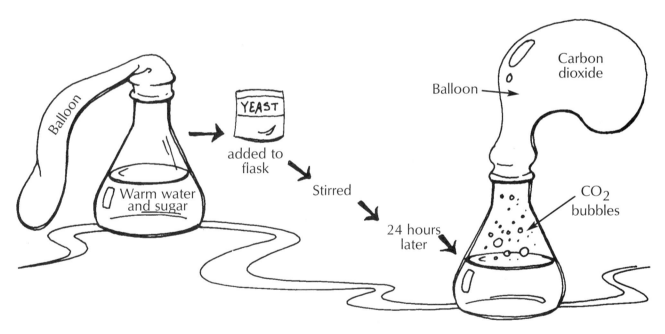

You can determine whether yeasts are alive by checking to see if carbon dioxide is produced. Indicators, such as bromthymol blue, can be added to the yeast mixture to check for the production of carbon dioxide. The indicator bromthymol blue changes color in the presence of carbon dioxide. The natural blue color of the indicator turns green or yellow if carbon dioxide is present. If no carbon dioxide is present, it remains blue.

Prelab Research Questions

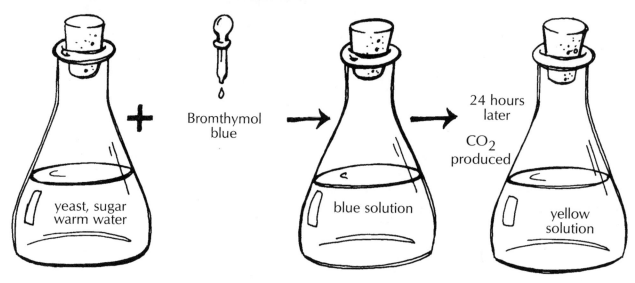

yeast, sugar
warm water

+

Bromthymol
blue

blue solution

24 hours
later

CO_2
produced

yellow
solution

Conduct library research to answer the following questions.

1. Define *respiration*. What are the end products of respiration? _____
   _____
   _____
   _____

2. Define *indicator*. Name an indicator besides bromthymol blue. What does the
   indicator you named detect? _____
   _____
   _____

3. Yeast is a unicellular fungus. Name three multicellular fungi. _____
   _____

4. What composes the cell wall of fungi? _____

5. Name two fungi that can cause disease or problems for humans. _____
   _____

The Effect of Pollutants on Yeast

Purpose: Determine the effect of pollutants on yeast.

Materials Needed:
Living yeast culture (consists of one envelope of yeast, 200 mL of very warm water, and two teaspoons of sugar)
Nonliving yeast culture (consists of one envelope of yeast, 200 mL of cold water, and two teaspoons of sugar)
Saltwater solution (29 grams of salt dissolved in 500 mL water)
Liquid soap solution (5 mL of liquid soap stirred into 500 mL water)
Six test tubes and stoppers
Two medicine droppers
Bromthymol blue
Test tube rack
Graduated cylinder
Wax pencil

Procedure:

1. Label six test tubes, A, B, C, D, E, and F.

2. Place 5 mL of the following in each specified test tube (see Figure 1).
   a. Living yeast culture in A, C, and E
   b. Nonliving yeast culture in B, D, and F

3. In test tubes A and B, add 5 mL of saltwater, add stoppers to the test tubes, and gently shake them.

4. In test tubes C and D, place 5 mL of soap solution, add stoppers to the test tubes, and gently shake them.

5. Do not add anything more to test tubes E and F.

Name _____

6. Add enough bromthymol blue to each test tube, so that the resultant color in each test tube is blue.

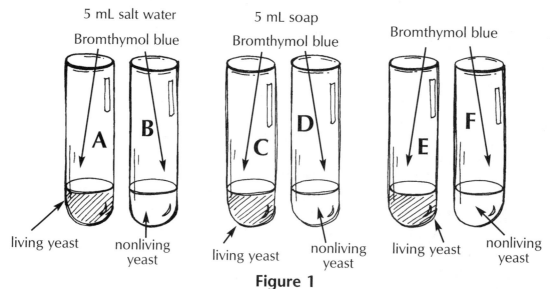

Figure 1

7. In the Data Table, write the word *blue* for each test tube under the heading, "Color of liquid at start of experiment."

8. Wait 24 hours.

9. Check each test tube and record the color in each test tube in the Data Table.

10. Dispose of your materials as your teacher directs you.

Data Table

	Color of liquid at start of experiment	Color after 24 hours
Test tube A		
Test tube B		
Test tube C		
Test tube D		
Test tube E		
Test tube F		

Letter to Fan of Fungi *from the Science Expert*

Use the information that you collected in the experiment that you just performed to write a response to Fan of Fungi's questions. Your letter should use complete sentences, correct spelling, and contain conclusions drawn from your experiment. You are now the science expert. Your letter should be creative and at least one to two paragraphs long.

Dear Fan of Fungi,

Sincerely,
Science Expert

Bird Bones

Dear Science Expert,

Last week I went to a family reunion. We had an awesome spread of food that day. I love all kinds of meat, so I ate tons of chicken and steak. When I finished I had a stack of bones on my plate that was embarrassing to my parents.

My aunt is a science teacher, so I tried to make good use of my bones by striking up a conversation about them. I picked up a chicken bone and a beef bone and remarked that there was definite difference in density here. Being a scientist, she asked if I could prove that statement. I told her to let me think on it and I'd get back to her.

Can you devise an experiment that will prove that the density of birds' and mammals' bones is different? Which will have the higher density? Help me save face with my aunt by sending me a response.

Sincerely,
Carnivore

Procedure

1. Read the Background Information: Bird Bones: Bone Density and Flight

2. Answer the Prelab Research Questions.

3. Follow the steps of the procedure to conduct the experiment following the Prelab Research Questions so that you become the science expert.

4. Acting as the science expert, write a response to Carnivore's letter.

Bone Density and Flight

Today three types of creatures soar through the air: birds, bats, and insects. Birds have several features that make flight possible. Feathers are one of the characteristics that allow birds the luxury of flight. A bird's feathers are lightweight and easily replaced if damaged. Even the first known bird, Archaeopteryx, had feathers and could fly. Archaeopteryx is now extinct (no longer living). This unique creature had characteristics of a reptile and a bird because it had teeth, a long tail, solid bones, and feathers. The link between it and modern birds is the existence of feathers.

What other features do modern-day birds possess that enable them to fly? The bones of birds are extremely light. In fact, the combined weight of a bird's bones is often less than that of its feathers. Many of the bones of birds are thin and fused together. The light weight of the bones along with their structure aids the feathers in making flight possible.

In the upcoming activity, you will determine how the density of a bird's bone compares with that of a mammal's. To determine density, you find the mass and volume of an object. Mass divided by volume gives you density. Mass can be obtained using a centigram balance, while volume can be calculated with the aid of a tall graduated cylinder and water. When an object is dropped into a known volume of water, the object will displace a certain amount of water, causing the water level to rise. The amount the water level rises in mL will be the volume the object occupied.

Name_____

Prelab Research Questions

Conduct library research to answer the following questions.

1. Define *mass* and *volume* and explain how they are related to density. _____
   _____
   _____
   _____

2. The bones of people are not hollow. What is the name of the material in our bones? What composes this material? _____
   _____
   _____

3. How many bones are in a human's body? _____

4. Do all birds fly? _____ If not, name one that does not. _____

5. Humans are mammals. Give some characteristics of mammals that are like those of birds and some characteristics that are unlike birds. _____
   _____
   _____

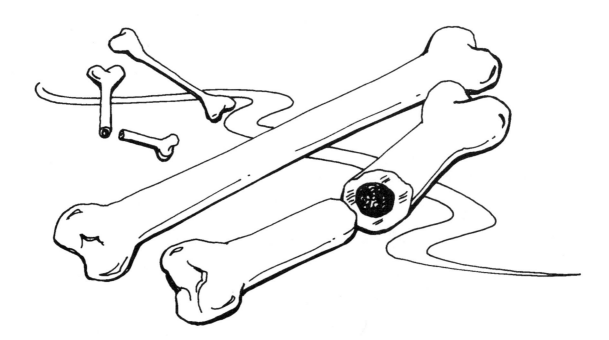

18

Bone Density

Purpose: Determine whether the density of a bird's bone is higher or lower than the density of a mammal's bone.

Materials Needed: Chicken bone (small enough to fit in a large graduated cylinder)
Beef bone (small enough to fit in a large graduated cylinder)
Triple beam balance
Water
Large graduated cylinder
Safety glasses

Procedure:

1. Use the triple beam balance to find the masses of a chicken bone and a beef bone. Record the mass of each in grams in the Data Table (see Figure 1).

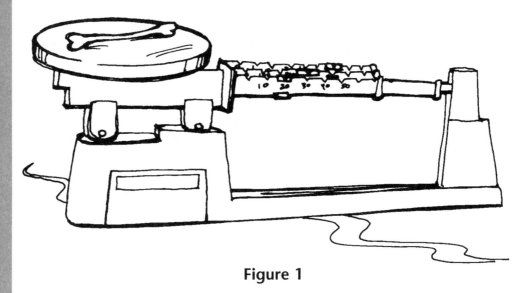

Figure 1

2. Place 30 mL of water in a graduated cylinder.

3. Drop the chicken bone into the water in the graduated cylinder.

4. The water level will rise. Read where the water level rose to and then subtract 30 from that number to find the mL of volume the chicken bone occupied. Record this number in the Data Table (see Figure 2).

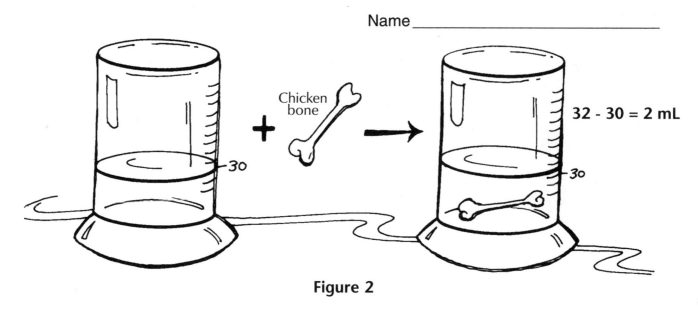

Chicken bone

32 - 30 = 2 mL

Figure 2

5. Pour the water and the chicken bone out of the graduated cylinder.

6. Fill the graduated cylinder to the 30-mL mark again.

7. Drop the beef bone into the water in the graduated cylinder and repeat step 4.

8. Find the density for each bone by dividing the volume the bone occupied in mL into the mass of the bone in grams. Record these numbers in the Data Table. Your answer will be labeled in grams/mL.

9. Dispose of the chicken and beef bones as directed by your teacher.

Data Table

	Mass	Volume	Density
Chicken Bone			
Beef Bone			

Letter to **Carnivore** *from the Science Expert*

Use the information that you collected in the experiment that you just performed to write a response to Carnivore's questions. Your letter should use complete sentences, correct spelling, and contain conclusions drawn from your experiment. You are now the science expert. Your letter should be creative and at least one to two paragraphs long.

Dear Carnivore,

Sincerely,
Science Expert

Green Factories

Dear Science Expert,

Each October I take a trip with my family to the Rocky Mountains to look at the leaves that have changed color. By the end of October, most, but not all, leaves have changed colors. My parents said that the chlorophyll had decreased and/or disappeared in the leaves that were no longer green.

Are my parents right about the chlorophyll? Can you perform a test that shows that the chlorophyll is really decreasing when the color of the leaves changes? Let me know the results of your test.

Sincerely,
Leaf Gazer

Procedure

1. Read the Background Information: Green Factories: How the Change in Seasons Affects Chlorophyll Content in Leaves.

2. Answer the Prelab Research Questions.

3. Follow the steps of the procedure to conduct the experiment following the Prelab Research Questions so that you become the science expert.

4. Acting as the science expert, write a response to Leaf Gazer's letter.

How the Change in Seasons Affects Chlorophyll Content in Leaves

In many places around the United States, the change in seasons can be seen through the color changes of leaves on the trees. In the fall or autumn, the leaves on many trees will change from green to orange, yellow, or red. Eventually, the leaves separate from the tree and drop to the ground.

The angle of the earth's axis and the earth's movement around the sun dictate the seasons of the earth. In the Northern Hemisphere, June 21 to September 23 is considered summer. During the summer, sunlight hits the Northern Hemisphere perpendicular to the earth's axis. This causes longer and warmer days. In the winter, the days are shorter and colder.

The approach of winter affects the behavior of animals. Some animals migrate to warmer climates, while others eat more food to add a layer of fat for insulation. The colder temperatures and shorter days also cause plants to respond in certain ways.

For example, deciduous trees change as winter approaches. Deciduous trees are those whose leaves change color in autumn and eventually drop from the tree. Chlorophyll, the pigment that gives leaves their green color, begins to diminish in autumn. As chlorophyll breaks down, other pigments can be seen. These now-visible pigments produce the yellows, reds, and oranges of autumn leaves. As the leaves change color, cells at the base of the leaf stem begin to weaken. Eventually, the stem cells die and the attachment of the leaf to the stem breaks. The leaf falls to the ground.

When all the leaves drop off the tree, food-making in the tree stops. At this point the tree is said to go into a stage of rest called *dormancy*. It will remain in that state until the longer days and warmer weather of spring appear once again. Spring will bring new cell and leaf growth.

Prelab Research Questions

Conduct library research to answer the following questions.

1. Define *deciduous tree.* Name one deciduous tree. _____

_____

_____

2. Name an animal who hibernates. _____

3. Other pigments in a plant are called *xanthophyll* and *carotene.* What colors are these plant pigments? _____

4. Explain the role of chlorophyll in plants. _____

_____

5. Define *photosynthesis.* _____

_____

Chlorophyll Content

Purpose: Determine the difference in chlorophyll content in green leaves and in leaves that have changed to their autumn color.

Materials Needed:
Two green leaves from a deciduous tree
Two leaves from the same deciduous tree that have already changed to their autumn color
Two tall glass containers
Filter paper
White paper
Pencils
Spoon
Rubbing alcohol
Clear tape
Scissors
Metric ruler

Note: This activity should be performed at the beginning of the autumn season.

Procedure:

1. Tear two green leaves into small pieces and drop all the pieces into a tall glass. Label this glass A.

2. Pour enough alcohol into the glass to cover the leaves.

3. Use a spoon to stir the leaves and press down on the leaves to extract the color from them.

4. Once the liquid takes on a dark tint, remove the spoon.

5. Cut a piece of filter paper so it is about 2 cm wide and long enough to extend from the top of the glass container to the bottom.

6. Tape the top of the piece of filter paper to the middle section of a pencil, so the strip hangs down from the pencil.

7. Lower the filter paper strip into the glass, so the pencil rests across the mouth of the glass. The filter strip should barely make contact with the liquid in the glass. If the filter strip dips too far into the liquid, readjust its position on the pencil (see Figure 1).

Figure 1

8. Leave the pencil and the filter paper in place until the liquid has been absorbed about three fourths of the way up the filter paper strip.

9. Remove the filter paper strip and tape it to a piece of white paper.

10. Observe the colors that have formed on the paper strip.

11. Repeat steps 1-10, but use two leaves that have begun to change to their autumn colors.

12. Compare the two strips.

Letter to Leaf Gazer *from the Science Expert*

Use the information that you collected in the experiment that you just performed to write a response to Leaf Gazer's questions. Your letter should use complete sentences, correct spelling, and contain conclusions drawn from your experiment. You are now the science expert. Your letter should be creative and at least one to two paragraphs long.

Dear Leaf Gazer,

Sincerely,
Science Expert

Keeping the Beat

Dear Science Expert,

I am an avid fisherman. Every Saturday morning I gather my fishing pole and my cup of earthworms and head to my favorite fishing hole. I love it when the bream are biting.

Last Saturday, I took three containers of earthworms with me on my trip. I carried one in my hands, left one container under the shade tree, and kept one in my ice box. As the day went by, the earthworms seemed to become more active, and it even looked like blood was flowing through their bodies more quickly than when I first arrived to fish. After I emptied the first cup, I used the cup from under the shade tree. These worms were not nearly as active as the first ones I used. By the end of the day, I had to use worms out of the cup kept in the ice box. These worms were the least active and acted like they were dead when I took them from the cup. Blood seemed to be flowing very slowly through their bodies.

I think the temperature had something to do with these observations. I believe that the pulse of the earthworm increases when temperature goes up. Is that true? Can you give me a little information on earthworm circulation and how it is affected by temperature?

Sincerely,
Gone Fishing

Procedure

1. Read the Background Information: Keeping the Beat: Blood Circulation in Earthworms.

2. Answer the Prelab Research Questions.

3. Follow the steps of the procedure to conduct the experiment following the Prelab Research Questions so that you become the science expert.

4. Acting as the science expert, write a response to Gone Fishing's letter.

Blood Circulation in Earthworms

Worms whose bodies are divided into sections are called *segmented worms.* These worms have the most complex body structures of all the worms. One common member of the segmented worm family is the earthworm.

Earthworms are found in moist soil. Earthworms tend to stay away from light, so they do not become dry. The best soil temperature for an earthworm is between 5 and 15 degrees Celsius.

If you examine the internal and external structure of an earthworm, you will find a body wall with muscle layers. The earthworm has both a mouth and an anus. Food taken into the earthworm passes through organs that grind and store food. Food is then sent to the intestines. The circulatory system of an earthworm consists of two blood vessels and ten hearts. The blood vessels run along the top of the body of the earthworm. If you look carefully, you can see them beneath the skin of the worm.

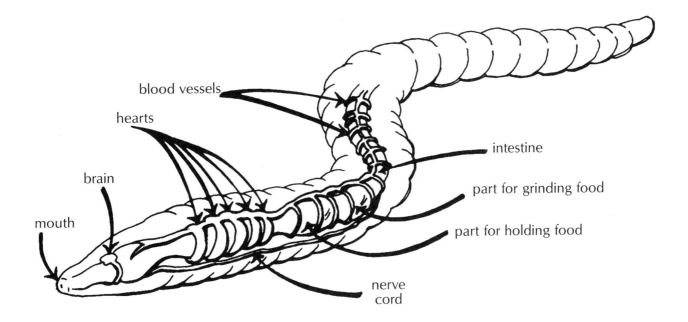

The earthworm's hearts pump blood through the blood vessels. The blood carries nutrients and oxygen to all tissues. If you look on the top side of an earthworm, you will see the blood vessels fill with blood and then empty. If you look near the earthworm's tail, you will see the blood vessel very clearly. The filling and emptying of blood is the pulse of the animal. You can even count how many times the blood vessels fill or empty in one minute. This pulse indicates how many times in one minute the earthworm's hearts pump.

Name_____

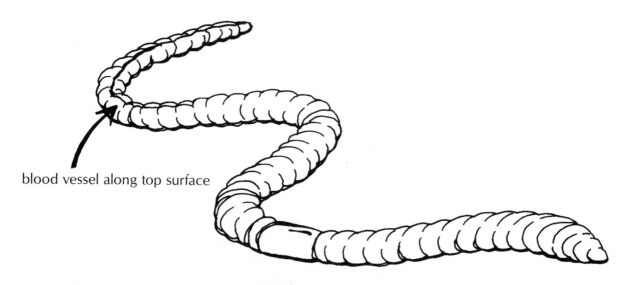

blood vessel along top surface

Prelab Research Questions

Conduct library research to answer the following questions.

1. Earthworms are in a group called *annelids*. Give characteristics of members of that group and name one more annelid member. _____

_____

_____

_____

2. The average pulse of a human is much higher than the pulse of an earthworm. How many beats per minute is the average human pulse? _____

3. An earthworm has a closed circulatory system. What is the difference between a closed and an open circulatory system? Which is the most efficient system?_____

_____

_____

4. Do earthworms have lungs? _____ How do they get oxygen into their bodies? _____

_____

_____

5. In a closed circulatory system, what organs cause pressure in the system? _____

_____

_____

EXPERIMENTAL PAGE
Temperature's Effect on Pulse

Purpose: Determine whether the temperature of the environment affects the pulse of the earthworm.

Materials Needed:
Three petri dishes
Magnifying glass or dissecting microscope
Stopwatch or watch with a second hand
Earthworm in a small beaker that has been suspended in water at 0° Celsius for 1 hour
Earthworm in a small beaker that has been suspended in water at 15° Celsius for 1 hour
Earthworm in a small beaker that has been suspended in water at 30° Celsius for 1 hour
Paper towels

Procedure: Note: Make certain that you do not harm the earthworm while you experiment. If you are uncertain of where the head and tail of the worm are located, ask your teacher to help you.

1. Gently move Earthworm A that has been in a beaker suspended in 0° C water to a petri dish. Wait for the worm to stop moving (see Figure 1).

2. Use a hand lens to locate the blood vessel along the top of the earthworm.

3. Using a watch with a second hand, count the number of times that blood fills and empties in a 60-second period. This will be the pulse of the worm. Record that number beside Trial 1 in the Data Table.

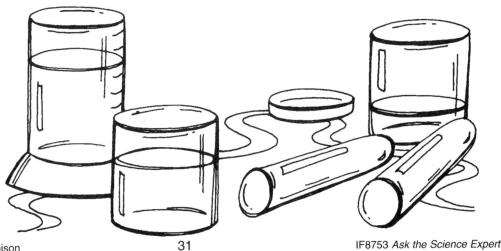

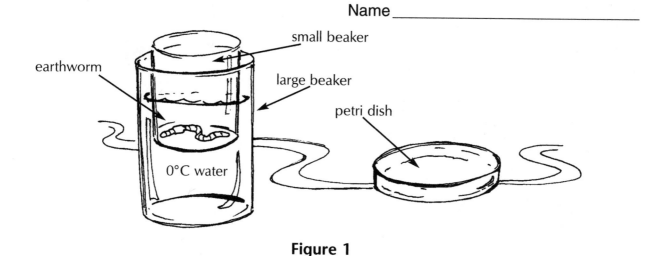

Figure 1

4. Repeat step 3 two more times with this earthworm and record your counts beside Trial 2 and Trial 3 in the Data Table.

5. Find the average of Earthworm A's pulse by adding the three trial values together and dividing by three. This number should be recorded by "Average" in the Data Table.

6. Place Earthworm A in the container your teacher designates.

7. Gently move Earthworm B that has been in a beaker suspended for one hour in water at 15° C to a petri dish. Wait for the worm to stop moving.

8. Repeat Steps 2-6 with Earthworm B.

9. Place Earthworm C that has been in a beaker suspended for one hour in water at 30° C to a petri dish. Wait for the worm to stop moving.

10. Repeat Steps 2-6 with Earthworm C.

Data Table

	Earthworm A at 0° C	Earthworm B at 15° C	Earthworm C at 30° C
Trial 1			
Trial 2			
Trial 3			
Average			

Letter to
Gone Fishing *from the Science Expert*

Use the information that you collected in the experiment that you just performed to write a response to Gone Fishing's questions. Your letter should use complete sentences, correct spelling, and contain conclusions drawn from your experiment. You are now the science expert. Your letter should be creative and at least one to two paragraphs long.

Dear Gone Fishing,

Sincerely,
Science Expert

Plant Perspiration

Dear Science Expert,

Is it true that leaves sweat? I saw a picture in my biology book of a baggie placed over a green leaf. There were little droplets of water inside the baggie. It looked like sweat. The caption under the picture said that the stomata let the water droplets escape. What are stomata? I was also wondering if trees growing in shady areas produced as much water as those in full sun? Can you shed a little light on that subject?

Sincerely,
Stumped on Stomata

Procedure

1. Read the Background Information: Plant Perspiration: Light and Transpiration.

2. Answer the Prelab Research Questions.

3. Follow the steps of the procedure to conduct the experiment following the Prelab Research Questions so that you become the science expert.

4. Acting as the science expert, write a response to Stumped on Stomata's letter.

Light and Transpiration

Plants take gases from the atmosphere and release gases into the atmosphere, as do people. Plant intake of gases, such as carbon dioxide and oxygen, takes place through small openings in the leaves called *stomata.* For photosynthesis (or food-making) to occur, the stomata of the leaf must be open. But when the stomata are open, the plant loses water. Two guard cells surrounding each stoma regulate closing and opening. The process of water loss through the leaves is called *transpiration.* Many factors in the environment, including temperature and light, influence the amount of water lost from plants.

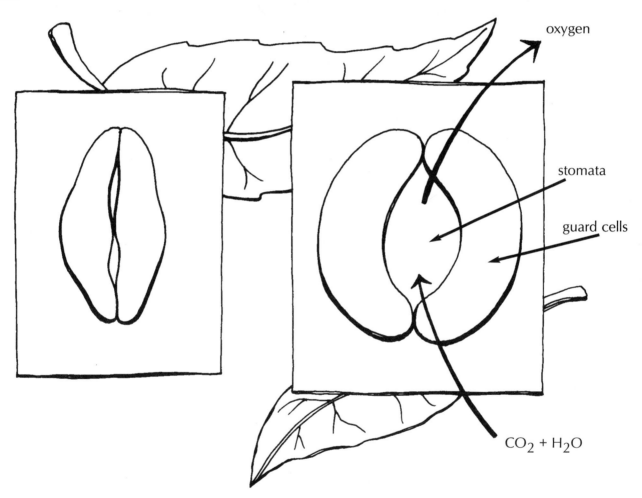

oxygen

stomata

guard cells

$CO_2 + H_2O$

The water lost during transpiration was supplied by the roots. Some large trees have leaves over 10 stories from the ground. How can the leaves at the top of these tall trees get water from the roots? The roots send the water through special passages called *vascular tubes* to the stems and leaves. Water is pulled up the tree because of the loss of water in the leaves. This need creates suction that draws the water up the vascular system.

Name_____

Prelab Research Questions

Conduct library research to answer the following questions.

1. Do the seasons affect the rate of transpiration? _____ How? _____

    _____

    _____

    _____

2. Explain the two properties of water that allow it to move from the roots up to the leaves of tall trees._____

    _____

    _____

3. Define *xylem* and *phloem.*

    _____

    _____

4. Define *turgid.* _____

    When are guard cells turgid? _____

5. Will trees transpire more in humid or dry conditions? _____

    _____

EXPERIMENTAL PAGE
Rate of Transpiration

Purpose: Determine how the amount of sunlight a plant receives affects the rate of transpiration.

Materials Needed:
Two large, clear plastic bags
Two pieces of string
Two small pebbles
A large beaker
A graduated cylinder
Two small deciduous trees (one in the sun and one in the shade)

Note: This experiment works best in the spring.

Procedure:

1. Select two deciduous trees of the same species and about the same size. One of these trees should be in the shade and one should be in the sun.

2. Begin with the tree in the sun. Select a limb on this tree that has the number of leaves typical of the rest of the limbs on that tree.

3. Count the number of leaves on the limb you selected. Record this number in the Data Table.

4. Count the number of limbs on the tree and record that number. Multiply the number of leaves on the limb by the number of limbs on the tree to find the approximate number of leaves on the tree. Record this number in the Data Table.

5. Place a pebble in the bottom of one plastic bag. Place the bag over the limb you chose, so the bag completely covers all the leaves on the limb. Use a string to secure the bag in place.

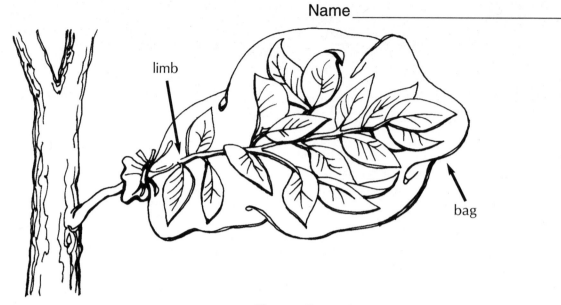

Figure 1

6. Repeat steps 2-5 with the tree you selected that was located in the shade.

7. Wait 24 hours.

8. Remove the bag from the tree in the sun. Punch a hole in the bottom of the bag and allow the water to run into the beaker.

9. Use a graduated cylinder to find the number of mL you collected. Record this number in the Data Table.

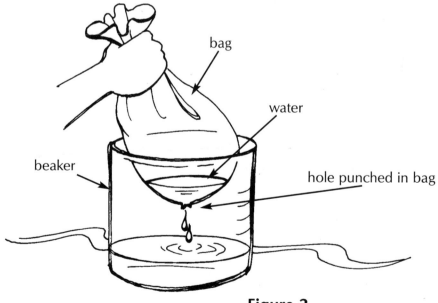

Figure 2

10. Repeat steps 8 and 9 with the tree in the shade.

11. Multiply the number of limbs on the tree located in the sun by the amount of water the bag contained. This number is the total amount of water transpired by the tree in a 24-hour period. Record this figure in the proper location in the Data Table.

12. Divide the total amount of water transpired in 24 hours by the total number of leaves on the tree. This number is the amount of water an individual leaf on the tree transpired in 24 hours. Record this figure in the proper location in the Data Table.

13. Repeat steps 11 and 12 for the tree located in the shade.

Data Table

	Tree in the sun	Tree in the shade
Number of leaves on test limb		
Number of limbs on tree		
Approximate number of leaves on tree		
Amount of water in bag after 24 hours		
Total amount of water transpired by tree in 24 hours		
Amount of water transpired by an individual leaf in 24 hours		

Letter to
Stumped on Stomata *from the Science Expert*

Use the information that you collected in the experiment that you just performed to write a response to Stumped on Stomata's questions. Your letter should use complete sentences, correct spelling, and contain conclusions drawn from your experiment. You are now the science expert. Your letter should be creative and at least one to two paragraphs long.

Dear Stumped on Stomata,

Sincerely,
Science Expert

Caffeine Drinkers

Dear Science Expert,

I drink 8-10 cups of coffee and tea each day. Sometimes I feel really nervous by the end of the day. My mother told me that it is the caffeine in the drinks that is causing me to be nervous. She also said that too much caffeine is bad for me. I know you can't test people and determine what effect caffeine has on them, but can you test plants and see the effect it has on seed germination? Write me back and let me know whether caffeine affects seed germination.

Sincerely,
Jittery Jack

Procedure

1. Read the Background Information: Caffeine Drinkers: The Effect of Chemicals on Living Things.

2. Answer the Prelab Research Questions.

3. Follow the steps of the procedure to conduct the experiment following the Prelab Research Questions so that you become the science expert.

4. Acting as the science expert, write a response to Jittery Jack's letter.

The Effect of Chemicals on Living Things

Chemicals can affect how living things function. *Depressants*, such as alcohol and narcotics, can slow down the nervous system. *Stimulants,* like amphetamines and cocaine, can speed up the nervous system. Some drugs, including nicotine, stimulate the nervous system first and then slow it later.

Chemicals in the form of drugs can be useful when used correctly. Doctors sometimes prescribe narcotics to give relief to people with pain. But chemicals can be harmful when used incorrectly. Smokers inhale cigarette smoke and nicotine. Continued years of smoking can result in lung diseases, such as emphysema and cancer. Women who drink alcohol while pregnant are at risk of giving birth to babies with birth defects.

Scientists discovered the connection between improper use of chemicals and disease by performing experiments in the laboratory. Since it is unethical and illegal to use human subjects for experimentation, scientists use other living organisms to test the impact of chemicals on life forms.

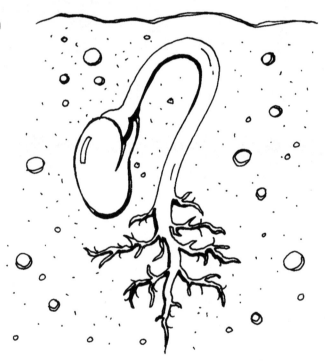

Plants can be used as the subject of experimentation. The percentage of seeds that germinate or "sprout" can be calculated during experimentation with plants to help evaluate the effect of certain chemicals on living organisms.

Prelab Research Questions

Conduct library research to answer the following questions.

1. List three or more factors that seeds require for germination. _____

   _____

2. Is caffeine a stimulant or a depressant?_____

3. Name two type of drinks that contain caffeine. _____

4. List some effects that caffeine has on the human body. _____

Does Caffeine Speed Up Growth?

Purpose: Determine the effect of caffeine on the germination of radish seeds.

Materials Needed:
Safety glasses
One hundred radish seeds
Four petri dishes and lids
A 10% caffeine solution (10 parts instant coffee combined with 90 parts water)
A 50% caffeine solution (50 parts instant coffee combined with 50 parts water)
A 90% caffeine solution (90 parts instant coffee combined with 10 parts water)
Graduated cylinder
Four pieces of filter paper
Scissors

Procedure:

1. Label the four petri dishes A, B, C, and D.

2. Use scissors to cut the filter paper into four circles that will fit in the bottom of each petri dish. Place a paper circle in all four petri dishes.

3. Dampen filter paper A with 5 mL of water.

4. Dampen filter paper B with 5 mL of 10% caffeine solution.

5. Dampen filter paper C with 5 mL of 50% caffeine solution.

6. Dampen filter paper D with 5 mL of 90% caffeine solution.

7. Place 25 radish seeds on each of the four pieces of filter paper in the petri dishes.

8. Cover the top of each dish with its lid and set the dishes aside for 24 hours.

A — in 5mL water

B — in 10% caffeine solution

C — in 50% caffeine solution

D — in 90% caffeine solution

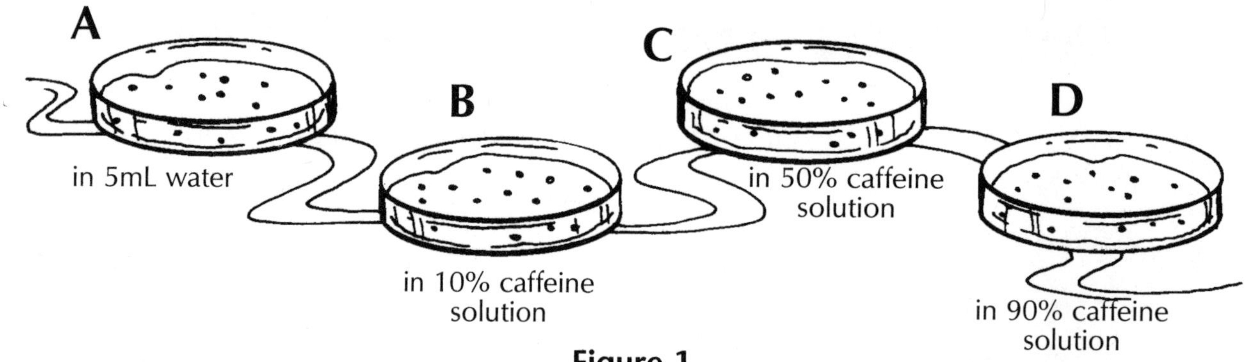

Figure 1

9. After 24 hours observe the seeds in each petri dish to see how many seeds have germinated. Record that number in the Data Table in the Day 1 column.

10. Add 5 more mL of the appropriate liquid to each petri dish, cover, and set aside for 24 more hours.

11. The next day, repeat step 9 and record the total number of seeds that have germinated in each dish under Day 2.

12. Repeat step 10 for 24 more hours.

13. Repeat step 11 and record results under Day 3.

14. Discard the contents of the experiment according to the directions of your teacher.

Data Table

Substance	Day 1	Day 2	Day 3
Water			
10% caffeine			
50% caffeine			
90% caffeine			

Letter to Jittery Jack *from the Science Expert*

Use the information that you collected in the experiment that you just performed to write a response to Jittery Jack's questions. Your letter should use complete sentences, correct spelling, and contain conclusions drawn from your experiment. You are now the science expert. Your letter should be creative and at least one to two paragraphs long.

Dear Jittery Jack,

Sincerely,
Science Expert

Baby Plants

Dear Science Expert,

My name is Freddy and I live in Canada. I've taken up farming as a hobby. I got a great deal on some radish seeds from a friend of mine at the Feed and Seed store. I'm ready to plant the seeds, but I have a few questions first. The temperature varies a lot from season to season where I live. Sometimes it drops 20-30 degrees below freezing, but in the summer it gets really warm.

Could you tell me if temperature is important in the germination of these seeds? I was wondering if I planted radish seeds in the cold weather if they would germinate as well as they do when the weather is warm. Any help you could give me would be most appreciated. I'm ready to put my seeds in the ground and watch them grow.

Sincerely,
Freddy Farmer

Procedure

1. Read the Background Information: Baby Plants: Seed Germination.

2. Answer the Prelab Research Questions.

3. Follow the steps of the procedure to conduct the experiment following the Prelab Research Questions so that you become the science expert.

4. Acting as the science expert, write a response to Freddy Farmer's letter.

Seed Germination

Have you ever eaten a seed? If you have eaten peas, beans, or peanuts, you have eaten seeds of plants. A seed contains a new plant and its stored food. If proper conditions are provided, the seed will eventually grow into an adult plant. The growth of the seed into a new plant is called *germination.*

You can open many seeds and see the small undeveloped plant inside. If you split a bean into its two halves, you will see the embryo of the plant. The embryo contains the future leaves, stem, and root of the plant. The remainder of the bean seed contains the stored food for the embryo.

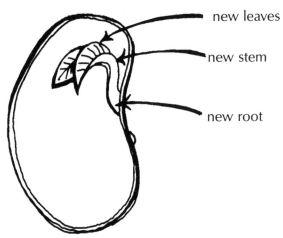

new leaves

new stem

new root

Germination of the seed requires the presence of certain things. Adequate moisture, temperature, and oxygen are a few factors that are necessary for the seed to germinate. The first visible evidence that the seed has germinated is the appearance of the root of the embryo.

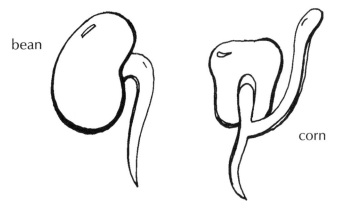

bean

corn

Water and oxygen are vital for seed germination. These two substances must penetrate the seed coat to start the process. Once water enters, the tissues of the seed swell. Eventually, the seed coat bursts. If water, oxygen, and other factors are supplied to the young plant, it continues to grow.

Name _____

Prelab Research Questions

Conduct library research to answer the following questions.

1. What is the function of a seed? _____

   _____

2. Where are the seeds on a conifer located? _____

3. The first seed plants on earth were gymnosperms. Today we have gymnosperms and angiosperms. How are they different as far as seed development goes?_____

   _____

   _____

   _____

4. What is the function of the part of the seed called the *seed coat?* _____

   _____

5. Where does the embryo of the seed get its nourishment? _____

   _____

Is Warmth Needed for Germination?

Purpose: Determine whether radish seeds require warm temperatures to germinate.

Materials Needed:
Two petri dishes
Paper towels
Scissors
Water
Sixty radish seeds
Access to an incubator and refrigerator

Procedure:

1. Label one petri dish A and label the other petri dish B.

2. Cut a paper towel into two circles. Fit a circle into the bottom of each of the two petri dishes.

3. Wet the bottom of the petri dishes so that the towels are moist.

4. Place 30 radish seeds on the paper towel in dish A and 30 radish seeds on the paper towel in dish B. Scatter the seeds so that they are not piled on top of one another (see Figure 1).

5. Put the cover on top of each petri dish.

6. Place petri dish A in an incubator to keep the seeds warm.

7. Place petri dish B in a refrigerator.

8. Each day for the next five days, observe your seeds to see if they have germinated. Each time you check the seeds, moisten your paper towel again. Each day record in the Data Table the total number of seeds that have germinated in each dish.

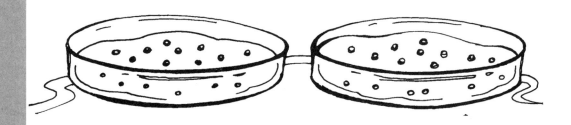

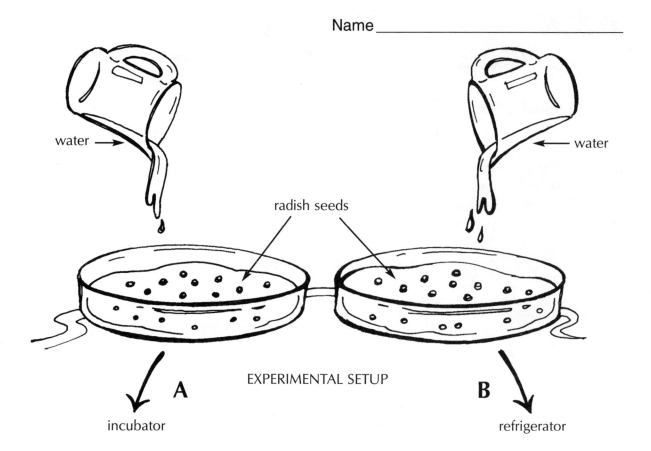

water →   ← water

radish seeds

EXPERIMENTAL SETUP

A   B

incubator   refrigerator

Figure 1

Data Table

# germinated seeds daily	Petri dish A (in incubator)	Petri dish B (in refrigerator)
Day 1		
Day 2		
Day 3		
Day 4		
Day 5		

Letter to Freddy Farmer *from the Science Expert*

Use the information that you collected in the experiment that you just performed to write a response to Freddy Farmer's questions. Your letter should use complete sentences, correct spelling, and contain conclusions drawn from your experiment. You are now the science expert. Your letter should be creative and at least one to two paragraphs long.

Dear Freddy Farmer,

Sincerely,
Science Expert

Facts About Fungi

Dear Science Expert,

Yesterday I started to make a ham sandwich, and there was green mold all over the bread. My mother said she probably should be keeping the bread in the refrigerator during the summer months. I guess molds must like warm temperatures.

I have never noticed mold growing on anything but bread. Can it grow on other food sources? One of my friends told me that mold and mildew grew on cardboard boxes in their basement after it flooded one year. Does mold grow more quickly when moisture is present? I am really curious about this subject. I hope you can help me with my questions.

Sincerely,
Sandwich Lover

Procedure

1. Read the Background Information: Facts About Fungi: Factors Affecting Mold Formation.

2. Answer the Prelab Research Questions.

3. Follow the steps of the procedure to conduct the experiment following the Prelab Research Questions so that you become the science expert.

4. Acting as the science expert, write a response to Sandwich Lover's letter.

Factors Affecting Mold Formation

Have you ever walked into an old house and thought it smelled moldy? You were probably correct in thinking that molds were residing there. Molds belong to a group of organisms called *fungi.* Fungi are organisms that cannot make their own food. They acquire food by feeding off once-living or living material. Most types of fungi are made of many cells, so they can be seen without a microscope. Some examples of multicelled fungi are mushrooms, molds, and mildews.

Fungi that feed on once-living material are called *saprophytes.* Shelf fungi, mildews, and molds belong to this category. Shelf fungi look like tiny shelves growing from the side of dead trees. Mildew can grow on things like damp leather boots. Remember that leather comes from an organism that was once alive. Mold can grow on top of bread or day-old coffee left in a cup.

Some fungi feed on things that are still alive. These fungi are called *parasites.* The fungus that invades your feet and toes and causes athlete's foot is an example of a parasitic fungus.

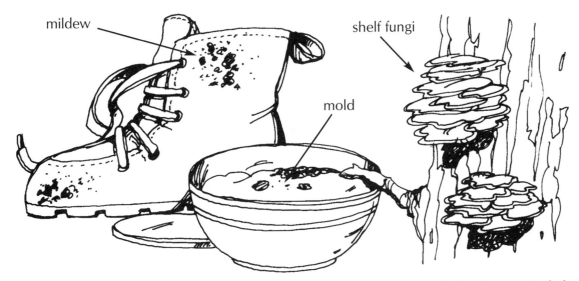

Fungi, like plants, grow better in some conditions than others. Bakeries control the growth of mold on bread by using chemicals. Certain chemical additives, such as calcium propionate, are applied to the bread to lengthen its shelf life. The addition of this chemical can help to delay the growth of mold on bread.

How do fungi get nutrition from a piece of bread? Mold grows from small structures called *spores.* Spores from the air land on the bread. The spores grow into the bread by means of branching root-like parts. Chemicals are produced by the mold that break the bread into usable material for the mold. The food passes into the cells of the mold by diffusion. If you magnify bread mold with a microscope, you will see root-like parts attached to a stalk. These root-like parts are embedded in the bread. On top of the stalk is a collection of spores. These spores are later released into the air to infect other food sources.

Name_____

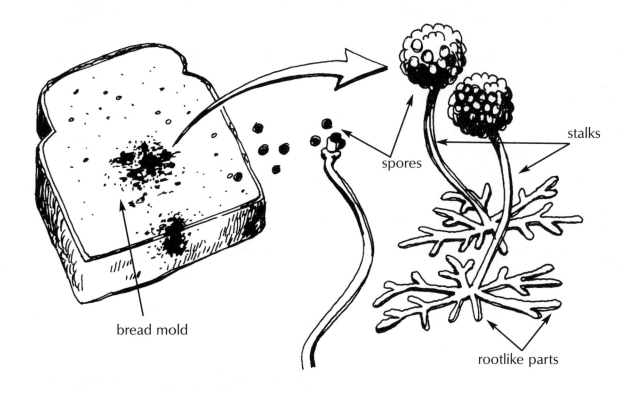

bread mold

spores

stalks

rootlike parts

Prelab Research Questions

Conduct library research to answer the following questions.

1. Name a fungus that has only one cell. State some of the uses of this fungus.

   _____

   _____

2. Do fungi have cell walls? If so, name the material from which they are made.

   _____

3. Define *mycorrhizae.* What is its connection to fungi? _____

   _____

   _____

4. A lichen is a fungus that lives in a symbiotic relationship with another type of organism. What is the name of that organism? _____

EXPERIMENTAL PAGE
Ideal Conditions for Mold

Purpose: Determine the food sources fungi can use when moisture is present.

Materials Needed:
Safety glasses
Six cotton swabs
Six jars with lids
Marking pen for jars
Potato flakes
Raisins
Two pieces of cardboard
Two or three pieces of moldy bread in a covered petri dish
Tablespoon
Graduated cylinder
Water

Caution: If you have severe allergies to mold, tell your teacher prior to the lab activity. She/He may want you to do an alternate assignment.

Procedure:
1. Label six jars A, B, C, D, E, and F
2. Place the following material in the designated jars:
   a. a tablespoon of dry potato flakes in jar A
   b. a tablespoon of dry potato flakes and 5 mL of water (stir) in jar B
   c. six raisins in jar C
   d. six raisins and 10 mL of water in jar D
   e. a piece of dry cardboard in jar E
   f. a piece of wet cardboard in jar F

3. Remove the lid from the petri dish with the bread mold. Rub a cotton swab over the mold on top of one of the pieces of bread to collect some mold spores. Now rub the swab with the spores you collected over the material in jar A. Cover jar A with its lid (see Figure 1).

4. Repeat step 3 using a new cotton swab each time and placing spores from the moldy bread on the material in the other five jars. Cover the jar with a lid each time.

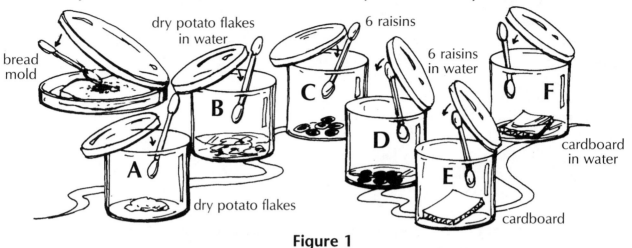

Figure 1

5. Store all covered jars in a warm, dark place.

6. Each day for five days, observe the contents inside the jars to see if mold is growing in the jar. In the Data Table, each day record your observations as to appearance of mold and amount of mold growth in each jar.

Note: Each day add a few drops of water to B, D, and F to keep them damp.

7. On day 5, dispose of the contents of the jars according to instructions from your teacher.

Data Table

Day	Jar A	Jar B	Jar C	Jar D	Jar E	Jar F
1						
2						
3						
4						
5						

Name _____

Letter to
Sandwich Lover *from the Science Expert*

Use the information that you collected in the experiment that you just performed to write a response to Sandwich Lover's questions. Your letter should use complete sentences, correct spelling, and contain conclusions drawn from your experiment. You are now the science expert. Your letter should be creative and at least one to two paragraphs long.

Dear Sandwich Lover,

Sincerely,
Science Expert

What a Response!

Dear Science Expert,

One of my favorite activities as a child was to play with pill bugs. I always called them "roly-polies" because they curled up in tiny balls when I plucked them from their home. I could find hundreds of these little creatures in the moist soil under the pine straw near my house. I would try to pick them up before they could curl into a ball. They were so quick that they usually curled before I could lift them from the ground.

In my science class, I am planning a class demonstration on the behavior of an invertebrate. I decided to experiment with pill bugs since I have a good supply of them near my house. I was wondering what pill bugs would do if you took them out of the soil and placed them on fabric. Do they prefer different types or textures of fabrics? I have some pieces of wool and silk my mother gave me. I want to know which fabric they prefer.

Sincerely,
Roly-Poly

Procedure

1. Read the Background Information: What a Response! Organisms and Their Responses to Stimuli.

2. Answer the Prelab Research Questions.

3. Follow the steps of the procedure to conduct the experiment following the Prelab Research Questions so that you become the science expert.

4. Acting as the science expert, write a response to Roly-Poly's letter.

Organisms and Their Responses to Stimuli

Everything an animal does is part of its behavior. Putting on a jacket when it is cold is part of your behavior. Behavior can be triggered by sense organs. Sense organs send messages about the external environment to other parts of an animal's body.

An animal's behavior is caused by a stimulus. For example, if a cat sees a mouse scurry across the floor, the cat races after it. The mouse is the stimulus. The cat chasing the mouse is the cat's response. All behavior begins with a stimulus that leads to a response.

stimulus

response = cat's movement

Stimuli are detected by some or all of an animal's sense organs. The eyes, ears, nose, skin, and tongue are some of the sense organs found in animals. A response to a stimulus usually results in contraction (shortening) of one or more muscles. This results in a change in the body position of the animal.

The behaviors of animals help them survive. Some behaviors help animals reproduce, find food, or protect themselves. The croaking of frogs brings them closer together so mating can occur. The way some animals avoid light helps keep them in dark, safe places. Living in packs or groups is a behavior that protects smaller animals from harm.

Name _____

Both complex and simple animals respond to stimuli. In this activity you will be working with invertebrates called *pill bugs*. Pill bugs are small animals that have a hard outer covering. They live on land but must stay in a moist environment to breathe through their gills. The pill bug is often found underneath logs, pine straw, or soil. It is most active at night when humidity is high.

When a pill bug is threatened by a predator (a stimulus), it curls up in a ball (a response). This protects its internal structures and its gills. It remains in this pose until danger has passed. Pill bugs will also respond to unsuitable environments. They will move from dry areas where it is hard for them to breathe to moister areas. They will also travel from cold places to warmer ones.

Prelab Research Questions

Conduct library research to answer the following questions.

1. An earthworm is an invertebrate. Describe how an earthworm responds to the stimulus light. _____

2. What type of sensory organs do earthworms possess that allow them to respond to certain stimuli? _____

3. Describe how an earthworm would react if threatened by a predator. _____

    _____

4. Where would you be most likely to find an earthworm? _____
    Why do they live in that environment? _____

5. Name three other invertebrates besides pill bugs and earthworms. _____

    _____

    _____

    _____

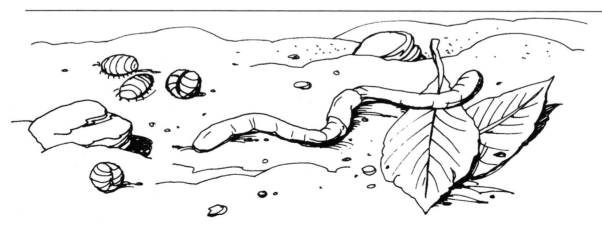

EXPERIMENTAL PAGE
Smooth or Rough?

Purpose: Determine whether pill bugs prefer an environment consisting of smooth or rough fabric.

Materials Needed:
Three pill bugs
Watch with a second hand
A petri dish (the bottom half only)
A small piece of silk
A small piece of wool
Scissors
Clear tape

Procedure:

1. Prepare your petri dish for the experiment by cutting your silk and wool samples so that one half of the petri dish is covered with silk and the other half is covered with wool.

2. Use clear tape to attach the pieces to the bottom of the petri dishes (see Figure 1).

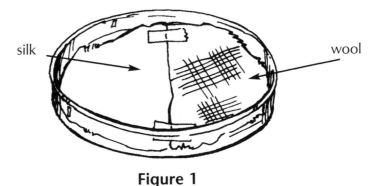

silk   wool

Figure 1

3. Place one of your three pill bugs in the center of the petri dish so it rests at the junction of the silk and wool (see Figure 2).

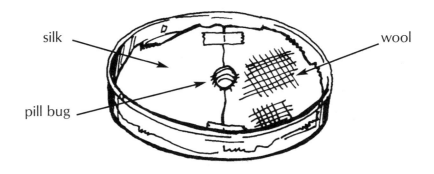

silk   wool

pill bug

Figure 2

Name _____

4. Watch and record the movement of the pill bug for the next five minutes. Record in the Data Table how many seconds the pill bug stayed on the silk and how many seconds it stayed on the wool. Also draw a diagram of the movement of the pill bug over the five-minute period. This will be done beside the row labeled Pill bug A.

5. Remove the first pill bug, and repeat steps 3 and 4 with a second pill bug. Record this information in the Data Table beside Pill bug B.

6. Remove the second pill bug, and repeat steps 3 and 4 with a third pill bug. Record this information in the Data Table beside Pill bug C.

Data Table

	Number of seconds on silk	Number of seconds on wool	Diagram of pill bug's five-minute trip
Pill bug A			
Pill bug B			
Pill bug C			

Letter to **Roly-Poly** *from the Science Expert*

Use the information that you collected in the experiment that you just performed to write a response to Roly-Poly's questions. Your letter should use complete sentences, correct spelling, and contain conclusions drawn from your experiment. You are now the science expert. Your letter should be creative and at least one to two paragraphs long.

Dear Roly-Poly,

Sincerely,
Science Expert

Speeding Up the Process

Dear Science Expert,

I play soccer every Tuesday and Thursday afternoon. Sometimes I get a little too aggressive and get an injury. Last Thursday I lunged at the ball and got a nasty cut on my lower leg. When I got home, my mother cleaned up the cut and put hydrogen peroxide on it. You should have seen the bubbles and foam. It was pretty amazing.

My mother told me that enzymes in my body were breaking down the hydrogen peroxide into water and oxygen. The bubbles indicated that oxygen was being produced. This process was cleaning my cut.

Since then I started thinking about enzymes. I read that meat tenderizer has enzymes that cause meat to get tender. I also read that many foods, like beef liver, contain enzymes. Will liver bubble when you drop hydrogen peroxide on it, like my skin did? How does increasing the temperature affect the action of the enzyme in the liver? Thanks for helping out with my enzyme mystery.

Sincerely,
Bubbling Body

Procedure

1. Read the Background Information: Speeding Up the Process: Enzymes and Reactions.

2. Answer the Prelab Research Questions.

3. Follow the steps of the procedure to conduct the experiment following the Prelab Research Questions so that you become the science expert.

4. Acting as the science expert, write a response to Bubbling Body's letter.

BACKGROUND INFORMATION

Enzymes and Reactions

All living systems contain enzymes. An enzyme is a special protein that speeds up chemical changes. The enzyme itself is not used up or changed in the process. All living tissues and their cells depend on enzymes for cellular reactions.

In your body, enzymes are at work each day. When you eat, your food must be digested. During this process, food is broken down into nutrients needed by the body. When you chew your food, this starts the digestive process. The grinding of the teeth against the food is called *mechanical digestion.* Enzymes then enter the process. Enzymes break complex molecules into simpler ones by a process called *chemical digestion.* An example of chemical digestion is the breaking down of carbohydrates into glucose. *Amylase* is an enzyme responsible for that reaction.

The shape of an enzyme dictates which substances it can affect. The shape of the enzyme fits like a puzzle piece into the shape of the molecule it affects. Because enzymes have specific shapes, altering their shapes affects their activity. Changes in the environment in which an enzyme is working can alter the activity of that enzyme. For example, if the pH (acidity/alkalinity) of the body is changed, an enzyme may not function appropriately. There are many other factors that can affect enzyme function.

Almost all chemical reactions produce hydrogen peroxide. This compound is damaging to the cell. As a result nearly all organisms contain an enzyme called *catalase.* This enzyme speeds up the reaction that breaks down hydrogen peroxide into the harmless products water and oxygen. During this reaction bubbles of oxygen gas are produced.

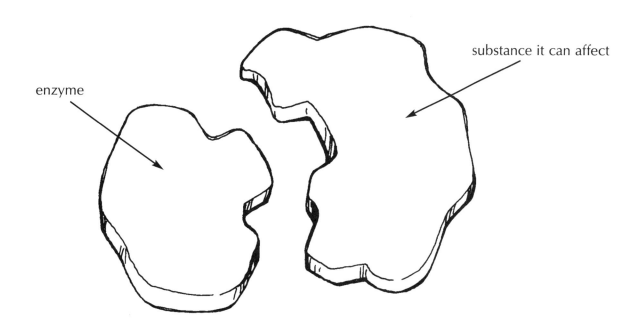

substance it can affect

enzyme

Name_____

Prelab Research Questions

Conduct library research to answer the following questions.

1. The enzyme *papain* is found in some food products. What is the name of the papain-containing common food product people use on meat?

   _____

2. Define *catalyst*. Why are enzymes examples of catalysts?

   _____

   _____

   _____

3. Enzymes are used in the production of certain foods. Name two foods that require enzymes in their production. _____

   _____

4. There are enzymes present in your mouth to break foods down to simpler molecules. Name the food types these enzymes work on and the name of the product they produce as a result of their action._____

EXPERIMENTAL PAGE

Active Enzymes

Purpose: Determine whether increasing the temperature affects the activity of an enzyme.

Materials Needed:
Safety glasses
Three large beakers
Six test tubes
Three pieces of beef liver (each about the size of a pea)
Hydrogen peroxide
"Hot hands" for handling hot beakers
Funnel
Test tube rack
Room-temperature water
Graduated cylinder
Water that has been heated on a hot plate to 37° C
Ice

Caution: Use the "hot hands" when handling heated glassware.

Procedure:

1. Label three beakers A, B, and C.

2. Place one pea-sized piece of beef liver into three test tubes. Place one test tube with the piece of liver into each beaker A, B, and C.

3. Place 5 mL of hydrogen peroxide in three more test tubes. Place one test tube with hydrogen peroxide in beakers A, B, and C.

4. Fill about one half of beaker A with ice, so that the test tubes rest in the ice. (Do not put the ice into the test tubes themselves.)

5. Fill beaker B about one-half full of room-temperature water. (Do not put water into the test tubes themselves.)

6. Fill beaker C about one-half full of 37° C water. (Do not put water into the test tubes themselves.) (see Figure 1).

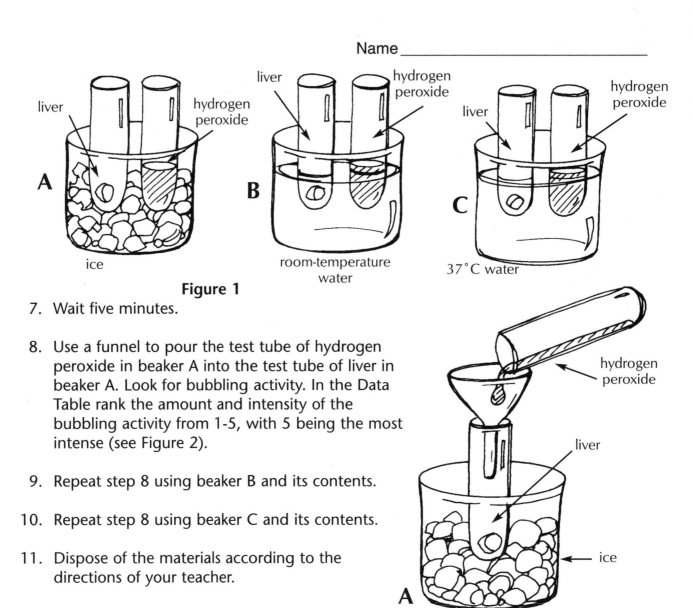

Figure 1

7. Wait five minutes.

8. Use a funnel to pour the test tube of hydrogen peroxide in beaker A into the test tube of liver in beaker A. Look for bubbling activity. In the Data Table rank the amount and intensity of the bubbling activity from 1-5, with 5 being the most intense (see Figure 2).

9. Repeat step 8 using beaker B and its contents.

10. Repeat step 8 using beaker C and its contents.

11. Dispose of the materials according to the directions of your teacher.

Figure 2

Data Table

	Rating of intensity of reaction (1–5)
Beaker A	
Beaker B	
Beaker C	

Letter to Bubbling Body *from the Science Expert*

Use the information that you collected in the experiment that you just performed to write a response to Bubbling Body's questions. Your letter should use complete sentences, correct spelling, and contain conclusions drawn from your experiment. You are now the science expert. Your letter should be creative and at least one to two paragraphs long.

Dear Bubbling Body,

Sincerely,
Science Expert

Polymer Savvy

Dear Science Expert,

I am in charge of ordering uniforms for our workers here at Oxley Industry. Most people just call me the uniform guy. Our company produces a bleach. The bleach in concentrated form can be pretty destructive to some fabrics. For the safety of our workers, we would like to order uniforms in a material that is comfortable but resistant to damage by bleach.

I have two uniform choices that fit our budget. I can order either uniforms made of polyester or ones made of wool. Wool seems like an odd choice, but it gets really cold in the factory. Could you do a little investigation and let me know which material would be the best to resist damage from bleach?

Sincerely,
Uniform Guy

Procedure

1. Read the Background Information: Polymer Savvy: Comparing Natural and Synthetic Polymers.

2. Answer the Prelab Research Questions.

3. Follow the steps of the procedure to conduct the experiment following the Prelab Research Questions so that you become the science expert.

4. Acting as the science expert, write a response to Uniform Guy's letter.

Comparing Natural and Synthetic Polymers

Plastics and synthetic (man-made) fibers are made of chains of small molecules. Each small molecule is called a *monomer.* A chain of linked monomers is called a *polymer.*

A polymer

monomer

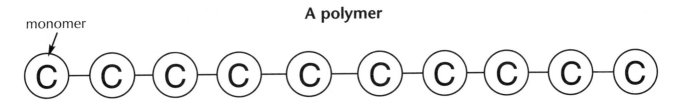

Polymers can be natural or synthetic (man-made). The structure of these two kinds of polymers is different. These differences give the polymers their properties. Some natural polymers are wool, cotton, and linen. Synthetic fibers, such as nylon, acetate, and polyester, became popular after World War II.

Man-made polymers are made of long, straight chains of monomers. These chains often line up side by side, causing the polymer fibers to be strong and to stretch easily. Unlike natural fibers, synthetic fibers do not break down easily. Some people feel that synthetic fibers are usually cheaper and wear better than natural fibers.

Many of the synthetic fibers were invented to replace expensive natural fibers. The clothing industry developed nylon to replace a natural fiber, silk. Silk, taken from the fiber of a silkworm cocoon, was expensive. The less expensive nylon lacked the softness of silk but was elastic and strong. For these reasons many women purchase nylon rather than silk stockings.

Polymers vary in properties of strength, flexibility, water absorption, and resistance to chemicals. The forces that bind together monomers of a fiber dictate their strength. If the forces between the chains of molecules are high, the polymer will be strong and hard to melt. Businesses and industries base their polymer selection on many of these properties.

Name_____

Prelab Research Questions

Conduct library research to answer the following questions.

1. What are *monomers?* _____

   _____

2. What are *isomers?* _____

   _____

3. What is a *hydrocarbon?* _____

   How is it related to a polymer?_____

   _____

4. Butane and methylpropane are isomers. They have the same formula. Find the formula._____

5. What does *organic* mean? _____

To Bleach or Not to Bleach

Purpose: Determine whether wool or polyester is more resistant to damage by bleach.

Materials Needed:
Safety glasses
Bleach
Two 250-mL beakers
Water
A small piece of light-colored wool
A small piece of light-colored polyester
Lab aprons (if available)
Masking tape
Magnifying glass
Paper towels

Caution: Do not put your nose over the bleach to inhale its vapors. Bleach can irritate the nasal and bronchial passages. Bleach spilled on clothing will discolor the clothing. If bleach gets on your skin, thoroughly wash your skin with water.

Procedure:

1. Label one beaker "wool" and one beaker "polyester."

2. Examine the fabric pieces with a magnifying glass. In the Data Table, indicate the condition of each fabric. (Does it have any holes? Does it have any stains on it?)

3. Place the piece of wool fabric and the polyester fabric in the beakers bearing their names.

4. Pour enough bleach over both pieces of fabric so that they are completely covered by the liquid (see Figure 1).

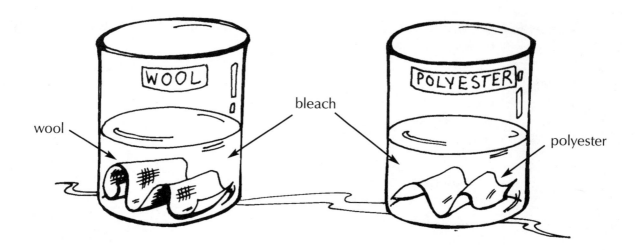

Figure 1

5. Wait 24 hours.

6. Pour the liquid out of each beaker and thoroughly rinse both pieces of fabric with water.

7. Use a paper towel to dry each piece of fabric.

8. Examine the pieces of fabric with a magnifying glass and record the condition of each piece of fabric in the Data Table. Note: Look for any holes or deterioration of the material.

Data Table

Fabric	Condition of fabric before addition of bleach	Condition of fabric after 24 hours in bleach
Wool		
Polyester		

Letter to Uniform Guy *from the Science Expert*

Use the information that you collected in the experiment that you just performed to write a response to Uniform Guy's questions. Your letter should use complete sentences, correct spelling, and contain conclusions drawn from your experiment. You are now the science expert. Your letter should be creative and at least one to two paragraphs long.

Dear Uniform Guy,

Sincerely,
Science Expert

Toxic Rain

Dear Science Expert,

I went with my family to the Statue of Liberty this past summer. It was pretty amazing to see it. The tour guide told us that repair work had been done on the statue because of exposure to saltwater and acid rain. The guide explained that the statue was safe now because the iron framework was protected. Copper covers the entire statue, so the iron inside does not rust or react with the environment.

I have thought about that a lot lately and wondered if acid rain affects a lot of buildings and statues. If things are not covered with a protective coating, will they begin to deteriorate? Can you tell me if acid rain adversely affects buildings and statues made of iron, plastic, aluminum, and marble? Thanks a lot for your help.

Sincerely,
Umbrella Toter

Procedure

1. Read the Background Information: Toxic Rain: Acid Rain and Its Effects.

2. Answer the Prelab Research Questions.

3. Follow the steps of the procedure to conduct the experiment following the Prelab Research Questions so that you become the science expert.

4. Acting as the science expert, write a response to Umbrella Toter's letter.

Acid Rain and Its Effects

Power plants and exhausts from automobiles release different gases into the atmosphere. Many of these gases contain sulfur. The sulfur combines with water vapor in the air to produce sulfuric acid. Rain and snow carry this acid back to the ground in the form of acid rain.

The impact of acid rain is most severe in the northeastern United States and in southeastern Canada. This is because these locations are downwind from coal-burning plants in the Midwest. These locations have acid levels almost 100 times greater than levels in other locations of North America.

The acid level is measured in units called pH (powers of hydrogen). The more acid a substance, the more hydrogen ions it releases. An *ion* is a charged atom. The pH scale ranges from 0 to 14. On the scale, seven is neutral. Below 7, substances are considered *acids.* Above 7 substances are called *bases.* The lower the pH number of an acid, the stronger the acid. The higher the pH number of a base, the stronger the base. Most places around the United States rarely have rainfall with a pH lower than 5.6. But in the northeastern United States, the pH of rain can drop below 4.

pH scale

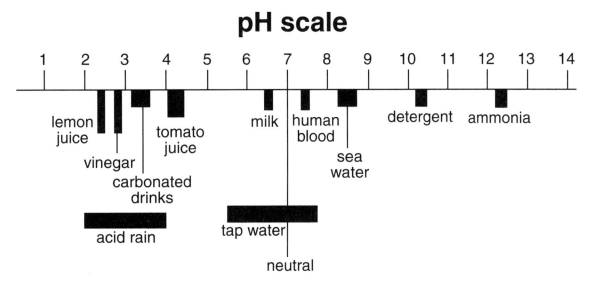

There is a very narrow range of pH in which living things can exist. If the pH of the environment becomes too high or too low, organisms will die. If the pH of soil becomes too low, certain types of plants will cease to grow. Acid rain can destroy life forms in ponds and lakes. This can occur when the pH of rain falls below 5.0 on the scale. Some species of frogs and other amphibians are becoming extinct because their young cannot develop in the acidic waters.

The pH of a substance can be measured by an indicator, a chemical that changes color at a specific pH. For example, hydronium test kits are indicators that can be used to show the exact pH of a liquid. If you dip a piece of hydronium paper in a liquid, the paper will change color. The color of the paper can be matched with a color scale that indicates the pH.

Name _____

Acid rain can also affect nonliving things like buildings and statues. In some places, the exteriors of buildings have been worn away and statues disfigured. This is because acids react with some building materials.

Prelab Research Questions

Conduct library research to answer the following questions.

1. The stages in the water cycle include *evaporation, condensation,* and *precipitation.* Define each of these. _____

_____

_____

_____

_____

2. Certain gases are released by the burning of fossil fuels that contribute to the formation of acid rain. Sulfur oxide is one of the gases. What is the other gas?

_____

3. When the pH of a lake becomes too acidic, scientists can correct this by liming it. What compound is used in liming and what purpose does this serve? _____

_____

4. On the pH scale, is an acid of 2 or 6 the stronger acid? _____

5. Besides hydronium paper, there are other indicators for acids and bases. Phenolphthalein is an indicator. What color does it change to when exposed to acids? _____ What color does it change to when exposed to bases? ____

_____

Determining the Effects of Acid Rain

Purpose: Determine which building structures are adversely affected by acid rain.

Materials Needed:
Three iron nails (not galvanized)
Three marble chips
Three small pieces of aluminum foil
Three small pieces of plastic
Twelve test tubes
Vinegar
Graduated cylinder
Safety glasses
Masking tape

Procedure:

1. Label four test tubes A, four B, and four C.

2. Place an iron nail in one test tube marked A, one marked B, and one marked C.

3. Place a marble chip in one test tube marked A, one marked B, and one marked C.

4. Place a piece of aluminum in one test tube marked A, one marked B, and one marked C.

5. Place a piece of plastic in the three remaining test tubes (see Figure 1).

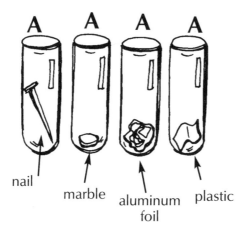

nail   marble   aluminum   plastic
                    foil

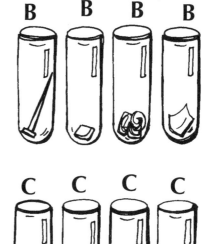

Figure 1

6. To all the test tubes marked A, no additional liquid will be added.

7. To all the test tubes marked B, add 5 mL of tap water. This will represent normal rain.

8. To all the test tubes marked C, add 5 mL of vinegar. This will represent the addition of acid rain (see Figure 2).

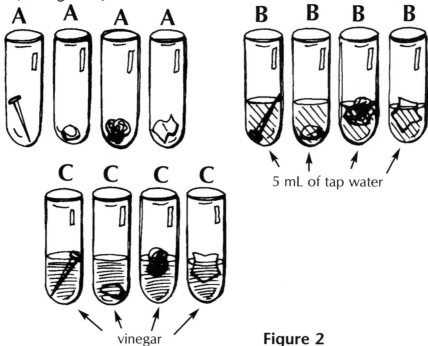

5 mL of tap water

vinegar

Figure 2

9. Wait 24 hours and observe if and how the materials in the test tubes have changed. Record your changes in the Data Table. If there were no changes, record "No Change."

Data Table

	Test tube A	Test tube B	Test tube C
Iron			
Marble			
Aluminum			
Plastic			

Name_____

Letter to **Umbrella Toter** *from the Science Expert*

Use the information that you collected in the experiment that you just performed to write a response to Umbrella Toter's questions. Your letter should use complete sentences, correct spelling, and contain conclusions drawn from your experiment. You are now the science expert. Your letter should be creative and at least one to two paragraphs long.

Dear Umbrella Toter,

Sincerely,
Science Expert

It's Freezing in Here

Dear Science Expert,

I love homemade vanilla ice cream. I have watched my Dad make it many times. I noticed that he pours salt on top of the ice around the canister of ice-cream mix before he begins to churn the mixture.

He told me that it helped to reduce the time required to solidify the ice cream. I noticed he never measures the amount of salt he pours on the ice. Does the amount of salt used affect the time required for the ice cream to freeze? Does a little salt work as quickly as a lot of salt?

Sincerely,
Sweet Tooth

Procedure

1. Read the Background Information: It's Freezing in Here: The Effect of Salt on Freezing Time.

2. Answer the Prelab Research Questions.

3. Follow the steps of the procedure to conduct the experiment following the Prelab Research Questions so that you become the science expert.

4. Acting as the science expert, write a response to Sweet Tooth's letter.

The Effect of Salt on Freezing Time

Have you ever helped your family make homemade ice cream? If so, you probably remember that the ice-cream mixture was composed of things like eggs, sugar, milk, vanilla, and salt. All this was beaten together and poured into an electric ice-cream churn that gently stirred the mixture as it rotated. The finished mixture was suspended within a container of ice.

The ice around the churn required one more item: salt. This substance was poured on top of the ice to help the mixture freeze quickly. In less than 30 minutes, the ice cream solidified and you were able to enjoy one of Americans' favorite sweet treats.

Have you ever wondered what salt has to do with the process of making ice cream? You already know that salt helps speed the freezing time of the ice cream. You may remember from science class that the freezing point of a substance is the temperature at which the vapor pressure of the liquid and solid are equal. Some substances, such as salt, lower the vapor pressure of water. Because salt lowers the vapor pressure of water, the vapor pressures of water and ice can only be equal at a temperature lower than that for pure water.

Name _____

Prelab Research Questions

Conduct library research to answer the following questions.

1. When you make homemade ice cream, you add ice and then churn the mixture in a container. Is the agitation necessary for the ice-cream process? _____
   Why? _____

   _____

   _____

2. The coldest temperature known is called *absolute zero.* Define *absolute zero.*

   _____

   _____

3. What is absolute zero in degrees Kelvin? _____

   What is absolute zero in degrees Celsius? _____

4. Most liquids will expand when heated. There is one liquid that expands when exposed to temperatures between 4 degrees and 0 degrees Celsius. What is the name of the liquid that does this? _____

5. Define *solute.* _____

   Define *solvent.* _____

   In a mixture of saltwater, name the solute and the solvent. _____

EXPERIMENTAL PAGE

The Effect of Salt on Freezing Time

Purpose: Determine whether increasing the amount of salt used in freezing an ice-cream mixture decreases the amount of time required for freezing.

Materials Needed: One gallon of ice-cream mixture (made from 4 eggs that have been beaten, 2 cups of sugar, 4 cups of half and half, 2 tsp vanilla, ½ tsp salt, and 1 gallon of milk) for the entire class
Three small Zip-loc baggies per group
Three large Zip-loc baggies per group
Crushed ice
Table salt
Stopwatch or a clock
Graduated cylinder

Note: Students need to be placed in groups of three for this activity.

Procedure:

1. Place 120 mL of ice-cream mixture in each of your three small Zip-loc baggies. Seal the baggies.

2. Fill the three large plastic baggies one-half full of crushed ice. Label these three baggies as A, B, and C.

3. Pour table salt in the graduated cylinder until it reaches the 30-mL mark. Pour this salt on top of the ice in baggie A.

4. Place 120 mL of table salt on top of the ice in baggie B.

5. Place 240 mL of table salt on top of the ice in baggie C (see Figure 1).

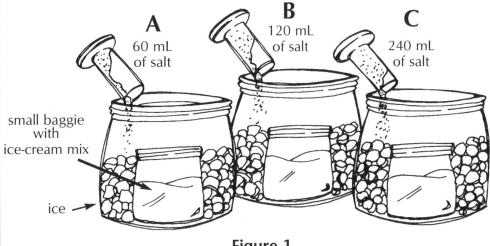

A 60 mL of salt

B 120 mL of salt

C 240 mL of salt

small baggie with ice-cream mix

ice →

Figure 1

6. Place a small baggie of ice-cream mixture inside each large baggie and seal the large baggie.

7. Each person in the group will be responsible for churning his/her baggie of ice cream by agitating the ice around the small baggie with his or her hands (see Figure 2).

8. Note the time on the clock when the churning process begins and continue until the ice-cream mixture has solidified. In the Data Table, record the number of minutes required for the mixture to solidify.

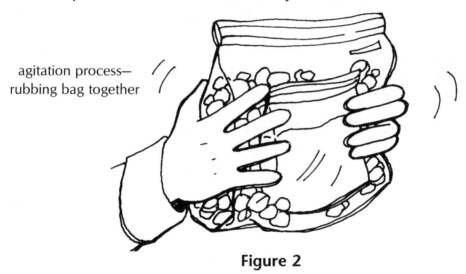

agitation process—
rubbing bag together

Figure 2

Data Table

	Time required for mixture to solidify
Bag A (30 mL salt)	
Bag B (120 mL salt)	
Bag C (240 mL salt)	

Letter to **Sweet Tooth** *from the Science Expert*

Use the information that you collected in the experiment that you just performed to write a response to Sweet Tooth's questions. Your letter should use complete sentences, correct spelling, and contain conclusions drawn from your experiment. You are now the science expert. Your letter should be creative and at least one to two paragraphs long.

Dear Sweet Tooth,

Sincerely,
Science Expert

Floaters

Dear Science Expert,

I love to go to the beach and watch the huge shrimp boats trolling out at sea. I stand on the dock and toss small pebbles into the ocean and watch them drop quickly to the ocean bottom. But the large ships stay afloat. I have even seen ships made of concrete stay afloat. I know it has something to do with the amount of water the ship pushes aside in the water to keep it from sinking.

While on vacation, my brother and I do a lot of swimming. Sometimes we swim in the pool at the motel and other times we go down to the ocean to swim. It feels great to float on your back with your face in the warm sun. I noticed that it seems like I can float a lot more easily in the ocean than at the pool. My brother thinks the same thing. If this is true, wouldn't ships of the same size be able to carry more heavy cargo in saltwater than in freshwater? Let me know if my thinking is on track or if I have just been in the sun too long.

Sincerely,
Water Lover

Procedure

1. Read the Background Information: Floaters: The Effect of Various Factors on an Object's Ability to Float.

2. Answer the Prelab Research Questions.

3. Follow the steps of the procedure to conduct the experiment following the Prelab Research Questions so that you become the science expert.

4. Acting as the science expert, write a response to Water Lover's letter.

The Effect of Various Factors on an Object's Ability to Float

If you have been to the ocean or a lake recently, you probably saw boats floating on the surface of the water. It is amazing that such heavy objects do not sink when placed on the surface of water. If you stood on the bank of a lake and tossed a golf ball into the water, what would happen to it? You know that it would sink. Even though a boat weighs much more than a golf ball, why does the boat float and the ball sink?

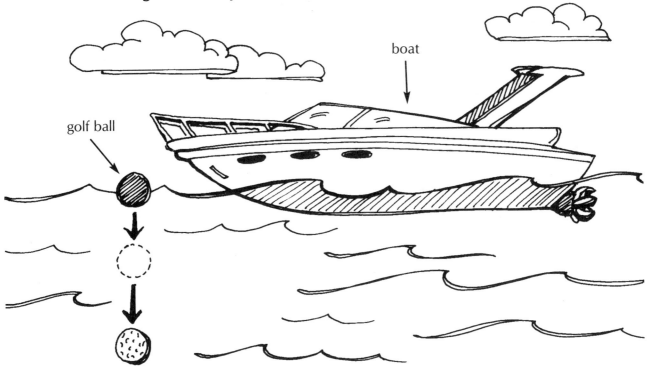

When you think of floating and sinking, think about a shoving match. The boat pushes or shoves down on the water below it. The water pushes or shoves back on the boat above. If the water pushes up harder than the boat pushes down, the boat floats. Even though a ship is very heavy, it is not as heavy as the water it pushes away. If the boat presses down with more force than the force with which the water pushes up, the boat sinks. Any object that sinks in water weighs more than an equal volume of water. The sinking object's weight is greater than the force pushing upward on the object.

The ability of a vessel to sink or float is dependent on many factors. The shape of the vessel is very important to its ability to float. Ship designers also consider whether the vessel will be in saltwater or freshwater, because this also affects the ease of floatation.

Name_____

Prelab Research Questions

Conduct library research to answer the following questions.

1. Define *buoyancy.* How is it related to density?_____

_____

_____

2. Explain the discovery that Archimedes made that relates to the information on the
   Background Information page. _____

_____

_____

3. What is the function of the swim bladder in a fish? _____

_____

4. What two things cause the density of ocean water to differ depending on the
   location?_____

5. Explain how a ballast in a submarine works to raise and lower the submarine.

_____

_____

_____

Sink or Float?

Purpose: Determine whether ships can carry more cargo and stay afloat more easily in saltwater or freshwater.

Materials Needed:
Scissors
A 0.5-M saltwater solution (29 grams of sodium chloride in 1,000 mL water)
Tap water
Ruler
Aluminum foil
Fifty pennies
A large beaker
Paper towels

Procedure:

1. Use scissors to cut a piece of aluminum foil 12 cm long and 12 cm wide. This will be the material you will use to make your boat.

2. Mold the aluminum foil into a boat-like structure with a hollow inside, so pennies can be added to the boat.

3. Fill the large beaker about three-fourths full with tap water.

4. Place your homemade ship on top of the water in the beaker.

5. Add pennies to the interior of your ship, one at a time until the ship sinks. Count the number of pennies you added just prior to the sinking of the ship. Record this number in the Data Table (see Figure 1).

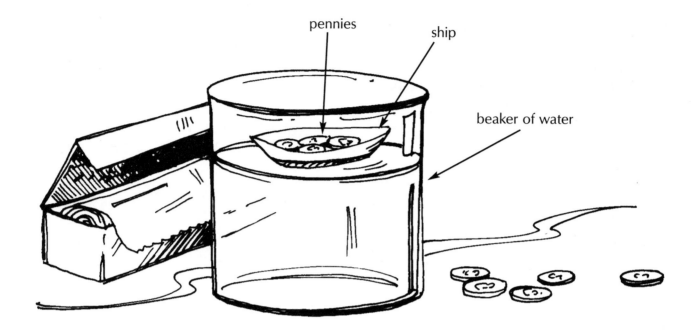

Figure 1

6. Retrieve your sunken vessel and dry it thoroughly.

7. Empty the tap water from the beaker and now fill the beaker about three-fourths full with saltwater.

8. Place your ship on the surface of the saltwater.

9. Repeat step 5.

Data Table

	Number of pennies added prior to sinking
Boat on freshwater	
Boat on saltwater	

Name _____

Letter to Water Lover *from the Science Expert*

Use the information that you collected in the experiment that you just performed to write a response to Water Lover's questions. Your letter should use complete sentences, correct spelling, and contain conclusions drawn from your experiment. You are now the science expert. Your letter should be creative and at least one to two paragraphs long.

Dear Water Lover,

Sincerely,
Science Expert

Free Fall

Dear Science Expert,

I am an avid skydiver. I love the sensation of jumping out of an airplane and falling through the air toward the earth. I also love the feeling I get when I pull the cord on my parachute, and the umbrella pops out as I drift gently toward the ground. When I jump with my other skydiving buddies, I notice that all our parachutes are shaped alike and made of the same type of fabric. Is the type of fabric used in making parachutes important in slowing the fall time?

Sincerely,
Bird Man

Procedure

1. Read the Background Information: Free Fall: Parachute Design and Skydiver's Fall Time.

2. Answer the Prelab Research Questions.

3. Follow the steps of the procedure to conduct the experiment following the Prelab Research Questions so that you become the science expert.

4. Acting as the science expert, write a response to Bird Man's letter.

Parachute Design and Skydiver's Fall Time

It may not seem like it, but air takes up space. When you pump air into a tire, the tire enlarges. The air entering the tire is being squashed, or compressed, into a small space. This compressed air has great strength and can support objects as large as trucks and automobiles. Large power tools like drills that penetrate concrete use compressed air to accomplish this feat.

Compressed air is also important in flying devices such as helicopters. It is the compressed air that helps the helicopter lift off the ground. As the blades on the helicopter spin, they push air downward. This squeezes the air under the blades and the compressed air pushes the helicopter upward.

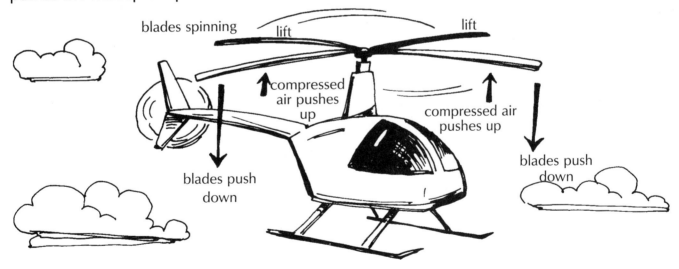

People who jump out of airplanes for sport are called *skydivers*. These individuals rely on their parachutes to lower them gently to the ground. The parachute must be designed so that it does not allow the person to fall to the ground too quickly. A fast descent can result in broken bones or even fatal injuries. The parachute functions by trapping air in the umbrella part of the parachute. The air is compressed inside the umbrella shape, so that it has a greater pushing power than the air around it. The compressed air presses upward and slows the descent of the skydiver.

Name_____

A lot of work and planning has gone into the design of today's parachutes. The type of fabric used is an important factor in making an effective parachute. The best fabrics must be lightweight but strong enough to trap and compress air. In the following activity you will be asked to determine which of four fabrics is the most appropriate to use for construction of a parachute in slowing the fall time.

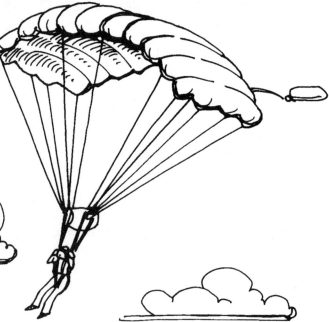

Prelab Research Questions

Conduct library research to answer the following questions.

1. Define *gravity.*_____

   _____

2. What is acceleration? _____

   _____

3. What is the number that represents acceleration due to gravity? _____

4. What is the role of friction in helping a person who parachutes from a plane to keep from getting hurt?_____

   _____

5. When a helicopter is hovering over a single location, what do you know about the force of gravity and air pressure beneath the helicopter? _____

   _____

   _____

Does Material Affect Fall Time?

Purpose: Determine whether the material used to make a parachute affects the fall time of an object.

Materials Needed: Scissors
Pieces of cotton, wool, nylon, and cotton-wool material
String or twine
Large washers (four per group)
Metric rulers
Compass (optional)
Stopwatch

Procedure:

1. Obtain a piece of each of the four types of fabric provided. Cut a circle that is 50 cm in diameter from each piece of fabric.

2. Cut 16 pieces of string that are 30 cm in length.

3. Attach four strings all around the edges of one of the pieces of fabric. Gather the four ends of the string together and tie them around a large washer (see Figure 1).

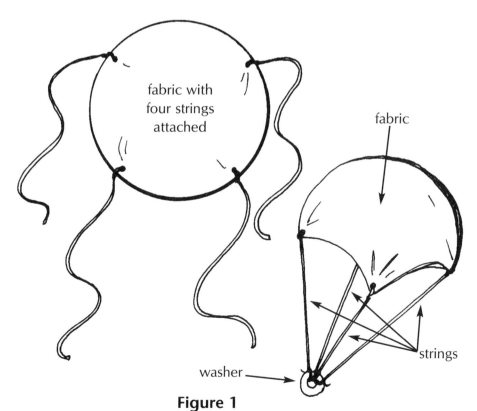

fabric with four strings attached

fabric

strings

washer

Figure 1

4. Repeat step 4 for the other three fabrics.

5. Drop one of the parachutes from the top of the gym bleachers to the floor while the fall time is determined with a stopwatch. Record the fall time in the Data Table.

6. Repeat this process for the other three parachutes.

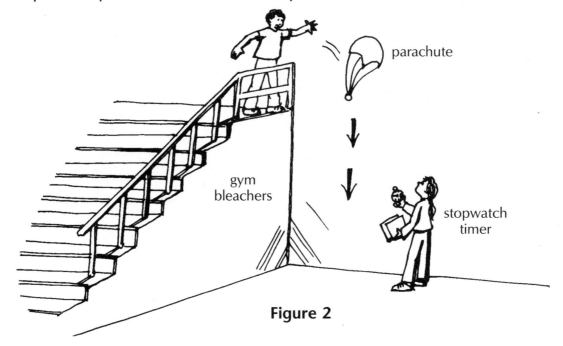

Figure 2

Data Table

	Number of seconds required for fall time
Parachute made of cotton	
Parachute made of nylon	
Parachute made of wool	
Parachute made of cotton-wool blend	

Letter to **Bird Man** *from the Science Expert*

Use the information that you collected in the experiment that you just performed to write a response to Bird Man's questions. Your letter should use complete sentences, correct spelling, and contain conclusions drawn from your experiment. You are now the science expert. Your letter should be creative and at least one to two paragraphs long.

Dear Bird Man,

Sincerely,
Science Expert

How Tall?

Dear Science Expert,

My friend and I have been trying to decide how tall the flagpole is outside our school. We even tried climbing it one night with a long tape measure to get its height, but I kept sliding back down to the ground before I reached the top. I know that there must be some way to find out its height without going to all that trouble. Let us know how to go about solving this mystery. Can you tell us the height of the flagpole outside of your place of business?

Sincerely,
Perplexed Pals

Procedure

1. Read the Background Information: How Tall?: Estimating Heights Scientifically.

2. Answer the Prelab Research Questions.

3. Follow the steps of the procedure to conduct the experiment following the Prelab Research Questions so that you become the science expert.

4. Acting as the science expert, write a response to Perplexed Pals' letter.

Estimating Heights Scientifically

Have you ever wondered how you could measure the height of a tall tree? If you could not use a tape measure, how could you accomplish this task? Actually, there are other ways to obtain the height of an object without actually climbing the object and measuring it as you go. These techniques produce approximations rather than exact numbers.

There are several ways of producing estimations of distances. One way you can accomplish this requires a ruler, a lab partner, and a measuring tape. In this activity you stand back from the object you are measuring. This time we will say that it is a tree. Have your partner stand by the tree. With a ruler in hand, extend your arm straight out in front of you. Back away from the tree that you are measuring, still holding the ruler straight in front of you. Continue to back away until the ruler and the tree appear to be the same height (see Figure 1).

Turn your ruler at a 90° angle so that it is parallel to the ground with the one end of the ruler appearing to be at the base of the tree. Have your partner walk away from the tree until he/she appears to be standing at the opposite end of the ruler. The actual distance between the tree and your lab partner is the approximate height of the tree. Use your measuring tape to find that distance (see Figure 2).

Figure 1

Name_____

Figure 2

In the upcoming activity, you will be estimating distances using a variation of this technique.

Prelab Research Questions

Conduct library research to answer the following questions.

1. What is the metric unit that is used to measure distance? _____

   What metric unit is used to measure long distances, such as those equivalent to miles? _____

2. What is the name of the prefix used with metric units that means 1/100? _____

3. The abbreviation SI is also known as the _____.

4. Indicate the metric unit (including prefixes) that would be most appropriate to measure each of the following values.
   a. diameter of a dime _____
   b. distance from the east to the west coast of the United States _____
   c. height of your classroom _____
   d. height of a microscope slide placed flat on the table _____
   e. your mass _____
   f. the contents of a thermos bottle _____
   g. the contents of liquid in an eyedropper container _____

Determining the Height of the Flagpole

Purpose: Determine the height of the flagpole located on your school campus.

Materials Needed:
Metric ruler
Measuring tape
Pencil
A flagpole
Calculator (optional)

Procedure:

1. Divide into pairs for this activity.

2. Find the height of one of the partners in the group. Record this measurement in cm in the Data Table by the name of the person.

3. The person whose height was taken should stand next to the flagpole (see Figure 1).

Figure 1

4. As you face the person next to the flagpole, slowly back away from her/him while you hold a pencil straight out in front of you at arm's length. Continue to walk backward from the flagpole until the pencil and your partner appear to be the same height (see Figure 2).

5. While still holding the pencil at arm's length, determine how many pencils are required to reach the top of the flagpole if you stacked the imaginary pencils one on top of another. Record the number of pencils required to achieve this in the Data Table (see Figure 3).

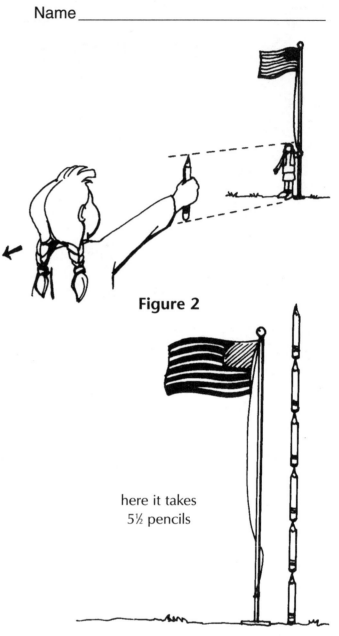

Figure 2

6. Multiply the number of pencils by the height of your partner. This will give you the approximate height of the flagpole. Record this information in the Data Table.

7. Switch roles with your partner and repeat steps 1-6.

8. Add the two heights of the flagpole together and divide by two to find the average of your calculations._____

here it takes 5½ pencils

Figure 3

Data Table

Name of partners	Height of person	Number of pencils to top of pole	Height of flagpole

Name_____

Letter to Perplexed Pals *from the Science Expert*

Use the information that you collected in the experiment that you just performed to write a response to the Perplexed Pals' questions. Your letter should use complete sentences, correct spelling, and contain conclusions drawn from your experiment. You are now the science expert. Your letter should be creative and at least one to two paragraphs long.

Dear Perplexed Pals,

Sincerely,
Science Expert

Falling

Dear Science Expert,

Every spring and summer my buddies and I spend lots of time at the swimming pool in our neighborhood. We like to play a game where we throw a golf ball into the deep end of the water and, when it hits the bottom of the pool, we all dive in and try to retrieve it. It seems to me that in the early spring the ball sinks more slowly than it does in the middle of the summer. I'm not sure if it is my imagination or not, but does temperature affect the speed with which an object sinks in a liquid?

Sincerely,
Dropping In

Procedure

1. Read the Background Information: Falling: Object Fall Time in Liquids.

2. Answer the Prelab Research Questions.

3. Follow the steps of the procedure to conduct the experiment following the Prelab Research Questions so that you become the science expert.

4. Acting as the science expert, write a response to Dropping In's letter.

Object Fall Time in Liquids

When you drop an object into a container of liquid, the object either floats, sinks slowly, or sinks quickly. This is determined by the properties of the liquid and the object being dropped into the liquid.

Density is a physical property that is defined as mass per unit volume. In simplified terms it is a measure of how tightly matter is packed. The measurement is usually expressed in units of grams per milliliter (g/mL). The density of pure water is 0.997 g/mL. Any object with a density greater than .997 g/mL sinks when placed in water, while objects with less density than water will float (see Figure 1).

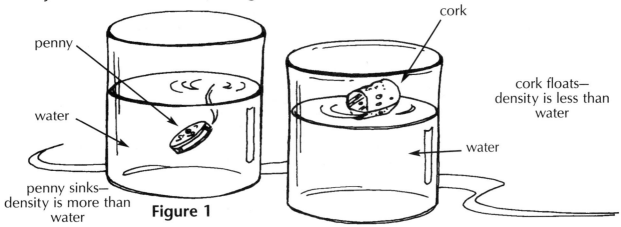

Figure 1

The greater the density of an object, the more quickly the object will sink in water. In other words, if you placed a piece of copper and a piece of gold of equal size and shape in a cup of water, the gold would sink more rapidly than the copper. This is because gold has a density of 19.3 g/mL while copper has a density of 8.94 g/mL.

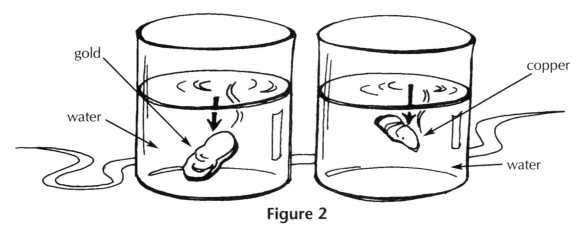

Figure 2

What happens if you place objects in liquids other than water? Not all liquids have the same density. Ethyl alcohol has a density of 0.789 g/mL. Some liquid substances, such as glycerine and corn syrup, have densities greater than water. This increased density affects the rate at which objects fall through the liquid. Substances will fall more quickly through alcohol than they will through higher-density liquids, such as glycerine and corn syrup.

Name_____

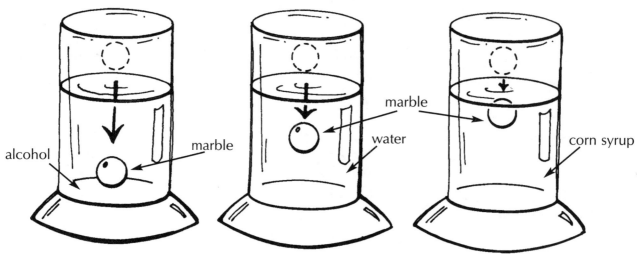

Figure 3

When testing the rate at which objects fall through a liquid, you must remember to use objects of the same shape and size and equal volumes of the liquid. It is wise to do at least three trials in an experiment and take the average of the three trials as the result (see Figure 3).

Prelab Research Questions

Conduct library research to answer the following questions.

1. Define *mass.* How does this relate to density? _____

_____

_____

2. Define *viscosity.* Is glycerine or alcohol more viscous?_____

_____

3. Think about what a cork does when placed in water. Compare the density of a piece of cork to the density of water. _____

_____

4. From what you have read about density, predict how the density of Styrofoam will compare to the density of water. _____

_____

Water Temperature's Effect on Speed

Purpose: Determine the effect that water temperature has on the speed with which an object falls vertically through a container of water.

Materials Needed:
Safety glasses
Three tall graduated cylinders or glass cylinders
Three marbles of equal size
A stopwatch
A 250-mL beaker
"Hot hands" (for handling hot glassware)
Water
Ice water
Hot water (boiled just prior to lab)

Procedure:

1. Label three graduated cylinders A, B, and C (see Figure 1).

2. Place 100 mL of room temperature tap water into cylinder A.

3. Place 100 mL of ice water in graduated cylinder B.

4. Place 100 mL of hot water in graduated cylinder C. **Caution: Use hot hands to handle the beaker with the hot water.**

5. Using a stopwatch, time how long it takes for a marble to drop through the water in each graduated cylinder.

6. Repeat each cylinder drop a total of three times and record your times in the Data Table.

7. After you have performed three drops in each cylinder, find the average time it took for the marble to complete its drop in each cylinder. Remember, to calculate the average, add your three trial values together, and divide by three.

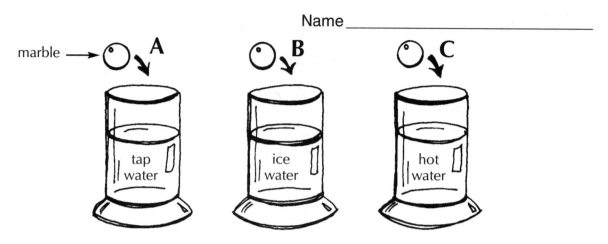

Figure 1

	Fall time in cylinder A (room temperature)	Fall time in cylinder B (ice water)	Fall time in cylinder C (hot water)
Trial 1			
Trial 2			
Trial 3			
Average			

swimming pool

Letter to Dropping In *from the Science Expert*

Use the information that you collected in the experiment that you just performed to write a response to Dropping In's questions. Your letter should use complete sentences, correct spelling, and contain conclusions drawn from your experiment. You are now the science expert. Your letter should be creative and at least one to two paragraphs long.

Dear Dropping In,

Sincerely,
Science Expert

Working for an Answer

Dear Science Expert,

I play basketball for my school. My science teacher is the coach. While we are at practice, he keeps telling us to work hard at running from one end of the court to the other. Some of the heavier guys on the team claim that they have to work harder than us "lightweights" to get up and down the court. Coach even agreed with them but told them not to complain and just put in the extra work.

Coach put in a special play called a "Power Surge." In this play everyone explodes at full speed down the court in a fast-break style. It is called the power surge because the success of the play is determined by how fast you travel down the court.

Some days I am not sure if I am at basketball practice or physical science class with all this work and power stuff. I was wondering if it is possible to calculate and compare work and power of different people. If so, can you calculate the work and power that a person generates in traveling in a round-trip from the science room to the office? If students traveled in groups of threes, would each group of students have the same average work and power? Thanks for your help. I want to impress my coach by showing him that I made the connection between basketball and science concepts.

Sincerely,
Power Surge

Procedure

1. Read the Background Information: Working for an Answer: Calculating Power and Work.

2. Answer the Prelab Research Questions.

3. Follow the steps of the procedure to conduct the experiment following the Prelab Research Questions so that you become the science expert.

4. Acting as the science expert, write a response to Power Surge's letter.

Calculating Power and Work

You are late and have to run from the gym to your third-period class. It takes you 30 seconds to run the 300-meter distance. Can you calculate how much work you did during your sprint and how much power you used? To accomplish this, you need one more measurement—your weight in pounds.

Work is the measure of the distance a force is moved. Work equals force times distance. *Newtons* are the measurements for force, meters measure distance, and *joules* are the measurements for work. To convert your weight to newtons, you multiply your weight in pounds by 4.45 N/lb.

During your sprint from the gym to your third-period class, you moved your body a distance of 100 meters. The force required to do that equals (your weight, 100 pounds, multiplied by 4.45) 445 newtons. So the amount of work done in this sprint was 445 N X 100 meters. You did 44,500 joules of work (see Figure 1).

If you weigh 100 pounds, you can convert this to newtons (the force you exert downward) by multiplying by 4.45 N/lb.
100 lbs x 4.45N/lb = 445 Newtons

Figure 1

W = F x d
W = 445 x 100 m   W = 44,500 J

Power is determined by dividing the work you did by the time required to accomplish the task. Units of time are measured in seconds and units of power are measured in watts. If it took 30 seconds to complete your sprint, you can calculate the power you used to accomplish the run. The work (44,500 J) divided by time (30 seconds) equals power (1,483 watts) exerted (see Figure 2).

Figure 2

Power = Work/time
P= 44,500J/30 sec   **P = 1,483 Watts**

Do you always do work when you exert yourself or raise your heart rate? What if you are trying to lift a 500-pound barbell off the floor? As you pull upward, you break out in a sweat, but the barbell does not move. You keep attempting this for 60 seconds. Have you done work? (see Figure 3)

Figure 3

Even though it seemed like you were working hard, you did no work. According to the definition of work, you must exert a force over a certain distance. Since you were unable to lift the barbell (500 pounds) any distance upward, you accomplished no work. You also generated no power, since no work was done.

Prelab Research Questions

Conduct library research to answer the following questions.

1. Name two conditions that must be met in order for an activity to be classified as work. _____

   _____

2. A weightlifter holds a 300-pound barbell over his/her head for three seconds in order to receive credit for an Olympic lift. Did the weightlifter do work? Explain your answer.

   _____

   _____

3. A machine makes work easier. Name two ways that machines accomplish this task for people. _____

4. Define *energy.*_____

   _____

5. Explain the difference between *potential* and *kinetic energy.* _____

   _____

   _____

Calculating Work

Purpose: Determine your group's average work done and power generated in a round-trip from your classroom to the door of the main office at your school.

Materials Needed: Stopwatch or clock with second hand
String
Tape measure
Calculator (optional)
Bathroom scale (optional)

Procedure:

1. Divide into groups of twos or threes.

2. List the names of all group members in the Data Table under "Names of group members."

3. Using the information provided in the Background Information, each group member should convert the number of pounds he/she weighs to newtons and record this number in the Data Table.

4. Stretch a string from your classroom to the door of the main office along the path you normally walk to get to the office (see Figure 1).

5. Use a tape measure or ruler to measure the length of the string. Multiply this by 2 because you will be making a round-trip. Record this number in meters in the Data Table for each person in your group under "Length of round-trip to office."

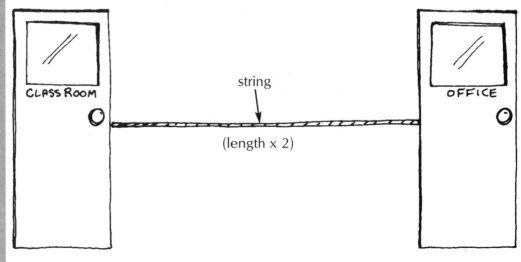

Figure 1

6. Each person in the group will walk at a normal pace from the classroom to the door of the main office and back while the other group member(s) use the stopwatch or a clock with a second hand to find the time required to complete this task. Record the time required for the trip in the Data Table in the appropriate location.

7. Each person in the group should now calculate the work he/she did and the power he/she generated. Use the formulas provided in the Background Information to help you do this. Record your calculations in the proper location in the Data Table.

8. Find the averages in each column by adding the three numbers (or number of people in your group) in the column and dividing by three (or whatever number of people were in your group). Record these calculations beside "Average" in the Data Table.

Data Table

Names of group members	Number of newtons of force	Length of round-trip to office (meters)	Time required to complete trip	Work done during trip	Power generated
Average					

Name_____

Letter to **Power Surge** *from the Science Expert*

Use the information that you collected in the experiment that you just performed to write a response to Power Surge's questions. Your letter should use complete sentences, correct spelling, and contain conclusions drawn from your experiment. You are now the science expert. Your letter should be creative and at least one to two paragraphs long.

Dear Power Surge,

Sincerely,
Science Expert

Smart Packaging

Dear Science Expert,

I have been reading some articles in science magazines about how companies are packing their merchandise with "peanuts" made of cornstarch. These are being used to replace Styrofoam "peanuts." It seems that the cornstarch materials decompose quickly in the environment.

I was reading about one experiment that used moist soil to test the decomposition time of packing materials. I was wondering if moisture in the soil influences the rate of decomposition of packing materials. If I buried newspaper and cornstarch "peanuts" in dry soil, would they decompose more slowly than if I used moist soil? Could you let me know the answers to these questions?

Sincerely,
Break Down

Procedure

1. Read the Background Information: Smart Packaging: Comparing Decomposition Times.

2. Answer the Prelab Research Questions.

3. Follow the steps of the procedure to conduct the experiment following the Prelab Research Questions so that you become the science expert.

4. Acting as the science expert, write a response to Break Down's letter.

Comparing Decomposition Times

In the United States a tremendous amount of waste is dumped in landfills. A large amount of this waste is in the form of packing materials for clothing, food, and other household items. As time passes, there are fewer places for waste to be deposited. People are being forced to come up with a way to slow the disposal process or recycle items that were previously placed in landfills.

More and more people have become involved in reusing and recycling materials previously classified as "trash." Many communities are sponsoring recycling or composting programs to decrease the amount of material disposed as waste. Items such as newspapers can be recycled to conserve trees. In fact, if all Americans recycled only one tenth of their newspapers, 25 million trees could be saved each year. We could also save a great deal of energy used to make paper from wood pulp.

recycling bin

Think of the last time a package was shipped to you. When you opened the box, the contents were probably surrounded by a packing material. The material was used to keep the contents of the box from being damaged during shipping. Packing material can take on a variety of forms. Some companies line their boxes with packing "peanuts," which may be made of Styrofoam or cornstarch. Other companies merely use paper products or plastic products to line the inside of the boxes. All of these items can be used to protect the contents of the box, but they differ in their impact on the environment.

The breakdown of a substance into its parts is called *decomposition*. Packing material that decomposes quickly is preferred over that which decomposes slowly. This is a consideration that many environment-friendly companies are taking into account.

Name_____

Cornstarch peanuts are environmentally friendly. This means that they break down easily in the environment. Many companies are using these cornstarch peanuts in place of the Styrofoam originals that did not break down in the environment.

Prelab Research Questions

Conduct library research to answer the following questions.

1. Explain the difference between renewable and nonrenewable natural resources and give two examples of each category. _____

_____

_____

_____

2. Differentiate between biodegradable and nonbiodegradable substances.

_____

_____

3. What do the symbols PET and HDPE stand for in the recycling industry? _____

_____

Also list one material that each is used to make. _____

_____

_____

4. Which of the following materials will degrade most quickly in the environment: cornstarch packing peanuts, Styrofoam packing peanuts, newspaper, or plastic?

_____

5. Name two organisms that cause organic material to decompose in the soil.

_____

EXPERIMENTAL PAGE
Decomposing Packing Materials

Purpose: Determine whether the presence of moisture is required for the decomposition of packing materials.

Materials Needed:
Safety glasses
Six cornstarch packing peanuts
Six small strips of newspaper
Four 250-mL beakers
Moist soil
Dry soil
Water

Procedure:

1. Label four beakers A, B, C, and D.

2. Place three cornstarch packing peanuts in beaker A and three in beaker B.

3. Place three strips of newspaper in beaker C and three strips in beaker D.

4. Completely cover the materials in beaker A and C with dry soil.

5. Completely cover the materials in beaker B and D with moist soil (see Figure 1).

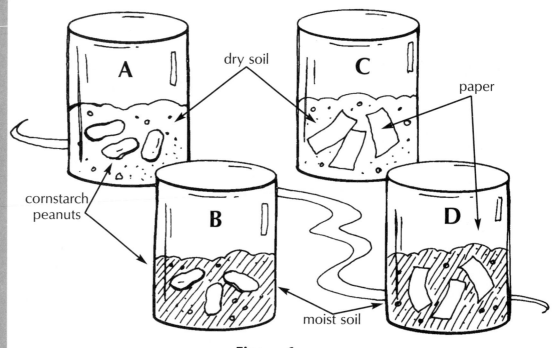

Figure 1

Name_____

6. For the next five days, leave the materials undisturbed except for adding water daily to the moist soil in beakers B and D to keep it saturated with water.

7. On day 5 empty the contents of each beaker and observe the condition of the materials buried under the soil. Record any changes in the condition of the packing materials in the Data Table.

8. Place the packing materials back in their appropriate beakers and recover with the soil. Wait five more days, making certain to add water to the moist soil daily.

9. On day 10 repeat steps 7 and 8.

10. On day 15 repeat steps 7 and 8.

11. On day 20 repeat steps 7 and 8.

12. Clean your lab materials according to the directions of your teacher.

Data Table

Appearance of packing material	Dry soil and cornstarch peanuts (A)	Moist soil and cornstarch peanuts (B)	Dry soil and newspaper (C)	Moist soil and newspaper (D)
Week 1				
Week 2				
Week 3				
Week 4				

Letter to Break Down *from the Science Expert*

Use the information that you collected in the experiment that you just performed to write a response to Break Down's questions. Your letter should use complete sentences, correct spelling, and contain conclusions drawn from your experiment. You are now the science expert. Your letter should be creative and at least one to two paragraphs long.

Dear Break Down,

Sincerely,
Science Expert

Answer Key

Teeth in Trouble

Prelab Research Questions

1. Deciduous teeth appear after birth and are temporary. Permanent teeth replace deciduous and last the remainder of a person's life.
2. dentin
3. It contains the blood vessels and nerves essential to nourishment of the tooth.
4. calcium and phosphorus
5. 32
6. 20
7. Teeth that do not oppose each other at the correct angle

The results of the student's experiment will reveal that small holes have appeared in the eggshell not covered with gel. The gel-coated eggshell should not have any holes in it. This shows that fluoride does protect the teeth from decay.

Little Beings
page 12

Prelab Research Questions

1. *Respiration* is the metabolic process by which an organism uses oxygen to convert the chemical energy in food into energy the body can use. End products are water, energy, and carbon dioxide.
2. *Indicators* are chemicals that indicate the presence, absence, or concentration of a substance. Answers will vary, but litmus paper indicates acids and bases.
3. Answers will vary but include mushrooms, mildew, bracket fungi.
4. It is made of chitin.
5. Answers will vary but include the fungus causing athlete's foot and molds and mildews causing allergies.

Students will find that test tubes B, D, and F will not change colors since the cultures were all dead. Test tubes A and C will not change colors because the pollutants killed the yeast. Only test tube E will survive and change color.

Bird Bones
page 18

Prelab Research Questions

1. *Mass* is the quantity of matter in a substance and *volume* is the space something occupies. Density equals mass divided by volume.
2. Humans have bone marrow in their bones. The marrow of a bone contains mineral salts, such as calcium and phosphorus.

3. 206
4. No. Answers can include penguin, ostrich, emu.
5. Most mammals give birth to live young and feed milk to their young. Birds lay shelled eggs and do not feed milk to the young. Both mammals and birds have a four-chambered heart.

Students will find that chicken bones have a lower density than beef bones, so a bird's bones are less dense than a mammal's bones.

Green Factories
page 24

Prelab Research Questions

1. Trees that shed their leaves. Some examples are oaks, elms, maples, beeches, dogwoods
2. Bear, squirrels, badgers, some insects
3. yellow and orange
4. Function in capturing sunlight so photosynthesis can occur
5. The process in which green plants produce carbohydrates and oxygen.

Green leaves will have more green color present on the filter paper than the leaves that have changed colors. Very little green will be found on the leaves that have already taken on autumn shades.

Keeping the Beat
page 30

Prelab Research Questions

1. Annelids have bodies with segments. *Annelid* means ring-like. Characteristics: Annelids have a coelem, which is a fluid-filled body cavity. Animals with a coelem have muscle around their body wall and around their digestive tract. The body of annelids is segmented or divided into sections. Examples include leeches and sandworms.
2. 72 beats per minute
3. In a closed system blood moves through blood vessels and never leaves the heart or the blood vessels. In an open system blood leaves this enclosed area. The closed system is much more effective because the blood is under great pressure and moves quickly through the vessels.
4. No. They get oxygen through the skin of their body
5. hearts

Warmer temperatures will accelerate the earthworm's heart rate.

Plant Perspiration page 36
Prelab Research Questions
1. Yes. Transpiration will be greater in the summer and spring than in autumn and winter.
2. Cohesion (binds to itself) and adhesion (binds to another object)
3. *Xylem* transports water while *phloem* transports dissolved sugars.
4. *Turgid*: being swollen with water. When the guard cells are turgid, the stoma is open.
5. Greater transpiration in dry air than humid air

Exposure to sunlight increases transpiration. The tree located in the sun should transpire more than the tree located in the shade.

Caffeine Drinkers page 42
Prelab Research Questions
1. Moisture, temperature, depth in the soil, composition of the soil, etc.
2. Stimulant
3. Answers will vary. Colas and coffee are two common ones.
4. Speeds up heart rate and metabolism and increases urinary frequency

Students will find that caffeine lowers the ability of seeds to germinate. The stronger the concentration of caffeine, the lower the germination rate.

Baby Plants page 48
Prelab Research Questions
1. Protect the embryo and help with seed dispersal
2. On the cones
3. The seeds of gymnosperms do not develop in a fruit, but angiosperms do
4. Protection of the seed
5. The food supply is inside the seed. It is similar to the yolk supplying food for the chick in an egg.

Radish seeds germinate better in warm conditions. Cold temperatures hamper germination.

Facts About Fungi page 54
Prelab Research Questions
1. Yeast. These fungi are used in making bakery products and alcoholic beverages.
2. Yes. Chitin
3. These are fungi that live on the roots of some plants and help the roots absorb minerals from the soil. The plants supply the fungi with carbohydrates.
4. alga

Students will discover that mold grows quickly on the objects in jars B, D, and F. Moisture is important for mold growth.

Provide a closed container at the end of the experiment for students to use to dispose of the contents of the jars.

What a Response! page 60
Prelab Research Questions
1. Earthworms will avoid light and go in the opposite direction in search of darkness.
2. They have a small brain in the anterior end of the worm and a well-developed nervous system that extends the length of the worm. Nerves in the epidermis of an earthworm detect touch and chemicals.
3. Earthworms will move away from the predator.
4. They live in moist soil and rarely appear during daylight. They need moisture to survive.
5. Answers will vary, but may include slugs, crickets, bees, centipedes, roaches, etc.

The results of the students' experiment should show that the pill bug will spend more time on the wool fabric than the silk. This is because the pill bug will associate the roughness of the wool with its natural environment of the soil.

Speeding Up the Process page 66
Prelab Research Questions
1. meat tenderizer
2. A *catalyst* speeds up a chemical reaction. Enzymes are catalysts in living things.
3. Answers can include some types of cheese, the soft center of candy, some meats, some brewing processes.
4. Enzymes in the mouth change starch to sugar.

Beaker C with its higher temperatures will show the greatest activity. Low temperatures can shut down enzyme function.

Polymer Savvy page 72
Prelab Research Questions
1. *Monomers* are molecules that make up a polymer.
2. *Isomers* are molecules that have more than one structure for a chemical formula.
3. A compound made of hydrogen and carbon is a *hydrocarbon*. Polymers are composed of hydrocarbons.
4. C_4H_{10}
5. Contains carbon

Students will find that the wool deteriorates overnight, while the polyester has not changed.

Toxic Rain   page 78
Prelab Research Questions
1. *Evaporation*—change from a liquid to a gas
   Condensation—change from a gas to a liquid
   Precipitation—the fall of rain or forms of water from the clouds to the ground
2. Nitrogen oxide
3. Adding calcium carbonate or limestone powder will neutralize the acid in lakes.
4. pH of 2 is the stronger acid
5. Phenolphthalein turns pink in acids and blue in bases

Student results should show that the test tubes with aluminum and vinegar, marble and vinegar, and iron and vinegar will show the appearance of bubbles and discoloration or degradation. The remaining test tubes will be unchanged.

It's Freezing in Here   page 84
Prelab Research Questions
1. Yes. Without agitation the freezing process would proceed too slowly to be practical.
2. Absolute zero is the temperature that makes a substance so cold that the particles that make up that substance do not move.
   There is no kinetic energy at this temperature.
3. 0 degrees Kelvin and -273 degrees Celsius
4. Water
5. A solvent is the material in which a solute is dissolved. In saltwater, the *solute* is the salt and the water is the *solvent*.

Increased quantities of salt result in faster solidification of the ice-cream mixture.

Floaters   page 90
Prelab Research Questions
1. *Buoyancy* is the tendency to remain afloat in a liquid or when the upward force that a fluid exerts on an object is less dense than itself. Density is mass per unit volume. The more dense an object, the more water required to make it buoyant.
2. He discovered the concept of density by sitting in a bathtub and witnessing an increase in volume of water, a result of placing his body in the water.
3. This organ allows the fish to rise and sink in the water.
4. The temperature of the water and the amount of salt in the water.
5. A submarine has nearly the same density as the ocean. A ballast tank fills and empties of ocean water to increase and decrease the density of the submarine, allowing it to rise and fall.

Students will find that more pennies can be added to the ship in the saltwater than in the freshwater.

Free Fall   page 96
Prelab Research Questions
1. *Gravity* is the pull of a body toward the earth.
2. change of speed during an interval of time
3. 9.8 m/sec/sec
4. Friction keeps the person from falling too quickly toward the ground and hurting himself/herself.
5. The air pressure must be equal to the force of gravity pulling down on the helicopter.

Students will find that the nylon material had the slowest fall time and was the most appropriate material for the parachute.

How Tall?   page 102
Prelab Research Questions
1. meter, km
2. centi
3. International System of units
4. a. mm or cm
   b. km
   c. m or cm
   d. mm
   e. kg
   f. liters or milliliters
   g. milliliters

Answers will vary. Evaluate student values for reasonable responses.

Falling   page 108
Prelab Research Questions
1. *Mass* is the quantity of matter in a body. Density equals the mass divided by the volume.
2. *Viscosity* is the degree with which a fluid resists flow under an applied force. Glycerine is more viscous.
3. Cork floats on water. It has a density less than water.
4. Styrofoam will float on water, making its density less than water.

Students will find that temperature affects the speed with which an object sinks. The hot water will allow the marble to sink most quickly. The marble in cold water will sink most slowly.

Working for an Answer   page 115

Prelab Research Questions

1. A force must be provided and an object must be moved a certain distance.
2. No. The object is not moved through a distance.
3. It helps to lessen the force required or it changes the direction of the force.
4. *Energy* is the ability to do work.
5. *Potential* energy is stored energy and kinetic energy is the energy of motion.

Students will have various measurements for work and power. The work measurements should be given in joules and the power measurements in watts.

Smart Packaging   page 121

Prelab Research Questions

1. Renewable resources are replaced by natural changes or ecological cycles. Hydroelectric, wind, and geothermal are renewable resources. Nonrenewable resources are not replaced by natural processes. Coal, gas, and oil are examples.
2. Biodegradable substances break down easily in the environment. Nonbiodegradable substances do not break down easily in the environment.
3. PET is polyethylene terephthalate and HDPE is high-density polyethylene. PET is used for carbonated beverages while HDPE is used in milk and juice containers.
4. Cornstarch peanuts
5. Bacteria and fungi in the soil

Students' results should show that moisture is necessary for decomposition. The materials in the dry soil will remain unchanged for the duration of the experiment.